Grace Psalms
In Psalms of Grace

Grace Psalms in Psalms of Grace

Joseph Phillips, Jr. M.Th.

Word in Due Season Publishing, LLC

Grace Psalms in Psalms of Grace
Joseph Phillips, Jr. M.Th.

Copyright © 2015 by Joseph Phillips, Jr.
All rights reserved

Word in Due Season Publishing, LLC
P.O. Box 210921
Auburn Hills, Michigan 48321-0921

Cover Design by Tywebbin Creations LLC
Mother Marion Wells' covder photograph courtesy of private collection.
Mrs. Phillip's Photograph by Mr. Eric Orlando Phillips

ISBN 13: 978-0-9829686-4-2.

Printed in the United States of America

No part of this book covered by copyrights hereon may be reproduced, stored in or introduced into a retrieval system, or transmitted, in any form, or by any means (electronic, mechanical, photocopying, recording or otherwise), without the prior written permission of the copyright owner.

All scripture marked KJV are from the King James Version of the Bible.

All scripture marked NASB are from the New American Standard Bible. Scripture taken from the New American Standard Bible, © Copyright 1960, 1962, 1963, 1968, 1971, 1972, 1973, 1975, 1977, 1995 by the Lockman Foundation. Used by permission.

All Scripture quotations, unless otherwise indicated, are taken from the Holy Bible, New International Version®. NIV®, Copyright ©1973, 1978, 1984 by International Bible Society. Used by permission by Zondervan. All rights reserved.

Word in Due Season Publishing, LLC supports the individuality of thought of every author. However, the thoughts, opinions, beliefs and expression of such in this work are solely the author's and do not necessarily reflect those of Word in Due Season Publishing, LLC and the publisher hereby disclaims any responsibility for them.

Dedication

As a prisoner of the Lord, I certainly give thanks to God for the gift of spiritual knowledge and understanding wisdom.

Blessed in devotional prayers, I wrote many of these Grace Psalms in Psalms of Grace to my mother while I was incarcerated. She read them diligently and encouraged me to put them in a book.

So herein, I now bless and honor my mother and father for their patience, love and direction.

Doris Mary Brantley Phillips

Table of Contents

Dedication 8

Acknowledgments 17

The Glory of the Gospel 20

A Testimony in Crisis and Calling for God's Deliverance 22

God's Gift of the Church 25

Jesus Breathes 27

In the Image of God 29

The Beauty of Holiness 31

Elect Lady 33

The Blessings of Our Heavenly Father 35

The Lamb of God 37

The Gift of the Church 39

God's Gift of Holy Faith 41

Hallelujah 43

Holy Anointed Oil 45

My Holy Father, My God 47

The Gift of Living Waters 48

The Ministry of the Holy Ghost 50

The Holy Kiss of the Holy Ghost 52

The Holy Resurrection of Glory	54
Grace's Covenant	56
God's Heart is Near	57
God is Our Lord	58
Gifted Children	59
Holy	61
Justice	63
God's Holy Spirit of Ministries Worship	65
God the Holy Ghost is our Authority of Justice	67
God's Holy Love	70
I, Too, Feel the Colours of the Wind	72
Spirit of Intercession	74
Tears of My Overflow	77
The Seasons of Love	79
Salvation is God's Gift to the Church	80
The Anointed Touch	81
Sin's Season	83
The Eye of Pride	85
Christian Suffrage in Spiritual Significance	87
Spirit of the Word	89
The Mother of Life	92
The Spirit of Hospitality	95

My Soul Praises	98
The Ministry of Miracles	100
God's Glorified Virtue	103
God Our Holy Father	106
The Father's Prayer	108
The Prayer of Faith	111
Holy Fire of the Holy Ghost	113
God's Wisdom Speaks	115
Spirit of Liberty	117
God's Gift of Praise	120
The Holy Seed of the Holy Ghost	122
God's Holy Passover Prayer	126
Life's Interlude	128
God is the Glory	129
The Spirit of Father's Day	133
The Father I Pray To Be	135
The Anointed of the Holy Spirit	137
God's Temple Endures Satan's Temptation	140
A Kiss in the Rain	142
I Know Secrets	144
The Pastor's Wife	145
God's Holy Gift	147

The Good Fight of Faith	150
God's Holy Light of Glory	152
Prayer	154
Jesus is the Way of the Spirit	155
A Faithful Hearer of God's Word Listens Obediently	157
God's Gift of Hope	159
Christmas Prayer	162
Fasting Faith	165
A Mother's Prayer on Mother's Day	167
The Virtuous Woman	173
Time	176
The Heart of Circumcision	179
The Circumcised Heart	180
Rainbows of Fruit	181
Who is the Shepherd and Savior of our Soul?	182
God's Glory of Restoration	185
God's Glory of Strength	188
Jesus Christ is Our Shepherd, Bishop and Savior	190
Jesus' Sacred Body	198
My Beloved Brethren	200
Prayer Dreamer	203
Prayer of Deliverance	206

Salvation	208
The Glory of Holiness	209
The Joy of God's Glory	214
The Preached Word	216
The Sacred Elect Elders	217
The Soul Keeper	224
Giving Your All to Christ	226
Inheritance	227
God's Holy Glory	230
Blessed Healing Grace	232
Heirs of Salvation	234
Holy Love	236
Logos	237
God is Love	239
Alphabetical Poem Listing	243
Biography	248

Acknowledgments

Through God's mercy, grace, and faith, I do pray in the acknowledgement of our Lord and Savior Jesus Christ; for Jesus Christ is our Bishop and Savior of our Soul. Truly, it is my sincere privilege to be a faithful believer and steward unto you our beloved members in the body of Christ.

In God's spirit of hospitality, and the mercies of grace, we welcome you, our fellow saints, family and friends. Special acknowledgment to my dear mother, Doris Mary Brantley Phillips and my wife, Victoria Ann Smith Phillips who encouraged me to bring these writings together in a book. I am thankful to have written such spiritual poems as Grace Psalms in Psalms of Grace. They are blessings to me unto eternal life for salvation in the kingdom of God. I thank Mr. Eric Orlando Phillips for his photography.

In the spirit of understanding and knowledge of God, God has helped me in these writings of Grace Psalms form repentance to redemption.

In the glory of God, I am yet learning the wisdom of God through the revelation of God's word. If it have not been for God's word in the Bible and the Spirit of the Holy Ghost and Jesus Christ, then these writings are without substance. This is truly an ultimate honor to receive God's blessings in becoming whole and delivered.

In my appreciation and my deliverance, I give thanks to God for being our true God of life. I also give thanks to God for my parents, my wife and children who are blessings onto God that I have a new life and new direction in the Word of God. May God bless you. Amen.

In the name of Jesus Christ,
His Servant, Joseph Phillips, Jr. M.Th.

Grace Psalms in Psalms Grace

The Glory of the Gospel

In the kingdom of God, God is the glory.

God's glory is fortified, sanctified and glorified.

The Holy Ghost fortifies the Word of God in the gospel.

For God is holy and God sanctifies His Word of Life.

For Jesus Christ is the glory of the gospel.

Who is thy holy crown of God's glory?

He is the seed of liberty by His obedience unto the Father's glory

And He is our prayer intercessor and advocate in all spiritual blessings

Where there is fortification, sanctification and glorification

In heavenly places.

There is sanctity in the Spirit of God and

There is sanctity in Jesus Christ's righteousness.

The crown of glory comes in the spirit of the gospel and

There is Holy Ghost power in the spirit of the Word.

God is the beauty of glory,

For Jesus Christ is the Word of glory.

For the glory of the gospel shields and nourishes thy soul.

The gospel answers and defends the truth.

Jesus Christ is the glory of the gospel,

For the beauty of the gospel is the word of holiness and the word of life.

The Holy Ghost gospel yields the fruit of perfection
And purification in wholeness.
Jesus Christ is the spirit of liberty who yields the goodness of deliverance.
Who blesses the poor and the meek in reliance to their faith in God?
Who heals the sick and mends the broken hearted from sin
Unto salvation and glorification?
Jesus Christ is the glory of the gospel. Amen.

A Testimony in Crisis and Calling for God's Deliverance

Dear God, I am holding onto my integrity and tenacity.

Then someone offers my daughter a gift unfitting to her size.

I immediately know her mother would not have given it to her

For the mother knows her size.

Suddenly, the zenith hour has come and to my greatest fear,

I was tested.

I perceive my troubles overshadowing me. I pray to God.

Why did you allow my marriage to end in divorce?

This was my greatest fear because God hates divorce.

There is no division between God and the Holy Ghost and

God and the Son, Jesus Christ.

Now, in my greatest fear, I perceive the highest panic and crisis.

My heart becomes overcome in heaviness and overflow with sharp pains.

Immediately, the light of heavens has darkened in a blazing fire.

The stars and sun surrender their lights.

Yet, they have turned away from me.

The oceans have become violent. She roars loudly in clashing thunder.

Her waves move swiftly in anger.

She creases until the edge cup risings circling over and over again and again.

How she hated me in her heart's fierce.

My sin has come to its peak and my soul is heavy in sin.

There in the eye of disobedience, my soul remains beaten and Weakened from the inner sin within and without.

Yet, my pride fills up and I fought my fears of sin's death.

But, I was made humble deeply and lowly.

I am full without me.

All my efforts were in vanity until my last breath of hope.

My spirit echoes and resounds for the life of God.

I have submitted unto the will of God.

I am relieved to call on God's name. My voice calls on the name of God,

"O save me, O God;

For the waters are come in unto my soul.

I sink in deep mire, where there is no standing:

I am come into deep waters, where the floods overflow me"

(Ps 69:-1-2 KJV).

O Lord, my sins against You are ever so great.

Why is there mercy upon me? For the inequity of my sin is ever before me.

My flesh is consumed by the heat of the fire.

The desires of idolatries in the body have come full.

My call for deliverance is voiced by Your will for me to be saved.

You alone are the pure way and the true light unto salvation.

You have repented my soul unto you for the mercy of reconciliation.

Please take my vessel, O Lord, my God. Take my sin of inequity away.

Please cleanse me deep in the river of God.

Please wash my soul where I shall magnify you forever.

Please purify me with a new heart.

Please create in me a perfect heart in the light of You, Holy Father.

Then, circumcise my heart to worship Thee and to praise

Thee all the days of my life.

May I please You, my Holy Father, God

To know your glory has over shadowed my spirit.

To serve You and to worship You in the fear of the Lord.

Thank you, Holy Father, for Your salvation and saving my soul.

I am freed in Your deliverance and I am saved.

For my testimony glorifies my Lord and Savior for being my deliverer

And hearing my call unto the spirit of liberty. Amen.

God's Gift of the Church

The church of our Lord, Jesus Christ is God's gift.

Blessed is Jesus Christ who is the gift to life

For He is the gift to the church.

Who is the Spirit of Christ the Anointed One?

The Holy Ghost is the gift of quickening powers of the spirit.

For the ministries of God are in the body of Jesus Christ

Who is the head of the church.

In the kingdom of God, there is virtue and victorious life in the church.

Where there is unity of the spirit in the body of Christ,

God ministers fellowship with the saints of the church;

For the saints of the church are heirs of salvation.

Jesus Christ is the living waters of life.

He is God's well spring of hope and trust in God's holy Word.

Who quickens and springs forth the fountains of living waters.

For the living Word is the Spirit of God.

Renews, restores, refreshes

And God is the Word of Life.

Repentance and redemption are gifts of the believer

To be relieved and saved.

There is victory in Jesus Christ.

Who tastes and knows the righteousness of

Jesus Christ by the Spirit of God.

For Christ triumphs over the enemy Satan, sin, and death.

Therefore, the church is sanctified in holiness

To be victorious in the virtue of God

Who comes in the spirit of love, hope, faith, grace, mercy and joy,

Meekness and peace?

In the spirit of hospitality, the gift of salvation

Welcomes you unto eternal life.

The gospel is the proclamation of salvation and

The foundation of the church.

In the spirit of holiness,

The gift of the church is to worship and to exalt God.

Jesus Breathes

Jesus breathes spirit unto my soul.

His consuming breath breathes life.

In the spirit of Liberty, I am free to breathe life.

The Lord our God weighs the heart.

Who offers the soul of life unto the fire of the Holy Ghost?

The Holy Ghost quickens the spirit with the unquenchable flame,

Flaming ministers in the fire of the Holy Ghost.

He opens my spiritual faith in my soul.

In worship prayers, my soul freely praises God.

Such spiritual fortitude fortifies the spirit to bless God.

God's eternal eyes look again, again, again

With power, honor and authority.

His sovereignty and supremacy reigns in authority.

His angel's spirit ministers through the flaming fire.

The Holy Fire of the Holy Ghost testifies His magnifying

Brilliances and glories through the radiant light of truth.

His presence glows and the Lord Jesus glorifies the Father.

In the fires of sanctification, redemption and purification,

My soul is forgiven by God.

From His power of forgiveness, the saint passes through the fire.

The Holy fire of the Holy Ghost is revealed by spirit and truth.

In the kingdom of God, the river of life flows eternally

Beyond the dreams of prophesy.

Spirit to spirit testifies in Jesus' gospel.

Jesus walks and talks to me though the eternal fire.

Jesus breathes in thy living soul. Amen.

In the Image of God

God created man in His own image.

In the power of creation, God says, "Let us create man in our own image".

Man is created in word and spirit to honor and obey God.

Man is crowned by the Spirit of the Godhead.

He is to have power over God's creation.

Through the power of the Holy Ghost, man is an inspired living soul.

In the spirit of liberty, man is ordained to please God,

To honor God, to satisfy God.

In the presence of God, the sacrifices of praise are given to delight God.

For man breathes the breath of God to worship and to praise Him.

In the spirit of truth, the sacred knowledge of God

Is given in loveliness and godliness.

God establishes His union of spiritual intimacy through prayer.

Man's relationship with God is the principal of life by His sovereignty,

Authority and supremacy.

In accordance to God's word, the heart of man is

Made of circumcision to obey God.

In the image of God, there is obedience in God's

Faith with a heart of circumcision.

By faith, man is created to pray in the Spirit of God.

There is spiritual significance in the spiritual identity of God.

Man is manifested in the glory of God to give his living testimony unto God.

In holiness, man's name glorifies God from his holy temple.

In the will of God, the unity of the Spirit remains with man.

As we call on God's name, we bless God with our

Whole soul and heart in spirit.

In the righteousness of Jesus Christ,

We worshipped in holy worthiness of God.

Jesus Christ bears thy godliness in the image of God who is

God's beloved son, Adam. Amen.

The Beauty of Holiness

Behold, God ordains the beauty of holiness

In the fear of the Lord, our God,

For worship is godliness and loveliness in the beauty of holiness.

For holiness inspires the adoration of God's love.

The ordination of peace rests in the spirit and holiness of Jesus Christ.

The Spirit of the Living God assures holiness is holy for

Jesus Christ is the crown of holiness.

Jesus Christ, the Son of God comes in the spirit of liberty and

The spirit of holiness.

Who is filled by the Holy Ghost, and clothed in the spirit of holiness?

Who is the gift of grace, faith, mercy, hope and justice?

In the Spirit of Christ, holiness remains in the fire baptism

Of the Holy Ghost.

Jesus Christ brings the Children of God into the

Right relationship of righteousness of God.

Repentance relieves our soul to believe in our Lord and Savior Jesus Christ.

For by Jesus' grace, we are saved through His faith which is the gift of God.

In the beauty of holiness, God redeems us to be the children of God.

And He declares us to be holy.

For the saint praises God in the beauties of holiness.

Behold, God is holy and God is love.

For God's word speaks unto our spirit and soul in thy prayers of love.

And the worshipper worships God in spirit and truth. Hallelujah.

In prayer, we have Holy Communion in worshiping and praising God.

God is holy in the beauty of love.

For the Word of God answers His love in the glory of God.

Behold, the Holy Spirit ushers in the beauty of holiness

In the presence of God

And the Holy Spirit sanctifies the children of God

In the spirit of hospitality.

Elect Lady

Blessed holy elect lady who is the bride of Jesus Christ.

Thy Holy Spirit is welcomed.

Who welcomes thee in the fruit of the Spirit,

Who adorns herself in the beauty of holiness.

For the beauty of holiness is glorified.

In the elect lady, thy bosom has fruit.

She is God's beloved heart in the fruit of the kingdom of God.

Thy beloved elect lady of God

The spirit of love is sanctified in Jesus' faith.

For salvation is thy eternal Holy Word.

To know God's Salvation covenant is to know thy gift of grace.

The holy elect lady who treasures everlasting

Life in Jesus' righteousness.

The anointed vessel of promise and honor.

So sweet in God's Spirit for edifying thy soul

Who is justified and glorified.

Edifying the living spirit in spiritual blessings in the body of Christ.

Holy lady elect, blessed be thy Lord, our God

Holy praises are freed in the living saints of love through

Jesus' healing virtue

Which springs forth the birth of grace and mercy in the

Love of truth by the fear of the Lord.

Hallelujah

Jesus' peace is secured. The elect lady is saved.

For this gift is salvation, the elect lady is prepared and ready,

Who is a ready bride for Christ Jesus.

Communion fellowship is welcomed.

The gospel is revealed and healed by God's

Words of faithfulness and fruitfulness.

To our God of truth is to know how great thy goodness in obedience is.

In the law of kindness, thy gift of salvation is

Blessed by the gospel of salvation.

Blessed elect lady of God who is sealed by His grace

Upon every word of God.

For she is clothed in His glory and strength.

To worship in holiness is to worship in spirit and truth.

Elect lady who rests in thy holiness and glory of salvation.

Blessed elect lady Amen.

The Blessings of Our Heavenly Father

In the kingdom of glory, our Heavenly Father's blessings
Are ordained and anointed.
Thy Holy Father God have hallowed His name,
For His name is blessed.
Marked by the blood of Jesus Christ, the Anointed One.

Blessed be God for God is blessed
And His blessings are to the heirs of the kingdom of God.
For God's kingdom reigns in the glory of truth.
For the Holy Spirit of our Father's blessings obeys God's Word.
He obeys God's commandment to bless the children of God through

All generation to generation and face to face
From the first fruit to thy last in the Spirit of Christ.
The kingdom of salvation is fruitful and multiple,
For God our Holy Father knows the intent of

His children's heart according to His will.
For the Holy Ghost is the ministry of God's blessings who is in the
Spirit of helps and in the spirit of holiness.
For the Holy Spirit prays for their souls to prosper.

He prepares their hearts and offers healing blessings.

He feeds and nourishes their souls in deep admiration.

And in inspiring warmth, He springs joy unto our hearts to worship God.

To worship God is to bless God with all your heart and all your soul and all your spirit.

To praise God is to honor God.

Bless God's holy name.

For the virtue of the spirit is the beauty of holiness.

In the fear of the Lord, God's presence is near through God's Holy Spirit.

God's name rings with lighten spirit.

The Lamb of God

Jesus Christ is the Lamb of God.

His faithful obedience is unto thy Holy Father, God,

Who is perfect in love and peace.

Who fulfills the sanctity of perfection; heart to heart and

Honor to honor for glory to glory.

Jesus Christ is our Savior and Bishop of our soul;

Who is the Lamb of God.

Who sacrifices the ultimate to bear witness for our sin and

To save lost souls.

The Lamb of God moves the grief of sins and the veils of death.

To believe in Jesus Christ is to be relieved in the sanctification of salvation.

The Lamb of God covers us in the kingdom of God by His righteousness

For the promise is fulfilled through the Lamb of God.

For Jesus Christ walks upon the waters of heaven and the waters of earth.

Who brings the fountain of joy in the living waters of life.

Who seeks the pure in heart through God's words and works.

Whose powers of the gospel are pure and true.

Whose bonds keep hold to the fire of grace

Through and by the power of the Holy Ghost.

To silence sin and to heal the sick in holiness and in the fruit of the Spirit.

Who answers truth in the spirit of the gospel and anoints the truth.

For the Lamb of God ordains peace and

Righteousness for justice and forgiveness.

In holiness, my soul lives and praises God because of the Lamb of God,

Our souls live. Amen.

The Gift of the Church

Jesus Christ is the gift of life and He is the gift to the church,

Who is the spirit of life in liberty and freedom.

Church life is victorious in the ministries of God.

The church's saints fellowship in God's ministry,

For Jesus Christ is the spring fountain of living waters.

For the victorious life church is sanctified in holiness by the

Spirit of love, faith, meekness, peace, and joy.

Who welcomes the gift of eternal life and the gift of salvation

From Jesus Christ who is our Shepherd and Bishop of our souls

By the prophesy and the promise of the Word of God.

For God is the Word of Life and the Word is the Spirit of God.

In God's love, there is victory in Christ.

"Blessed be the God and Father of our Lord Jesus Christ,
Who hath blessed us with all
Spiritual blessings in heavenly places in Christ" (Eph. 1:3 KJV).

Christ, who is the head of the church and the Savior of the church.

There is unity of the spirit in the body of the church in the kingdom of God

From edification to exhortation of praise, to worship and

To exalt God for forgiveness and reconciliation.

For Christ triumphs over the enemy, Satan, sin and death.

Christ, who conquers fears, hate and evil.

Overcomers are victorious in Christ.

Amen.

God's Gift of Holy Faith

Glory unto God who is ordained for His holy faith.

Saints are praying in the Holy Spirit to worship God in spirit and truth.

God's gift of holy faith is eternally anointed.

To please God is to have faith; faith to believe in His Word of Life;

For the Holy Spirit is the authority of faith.

God, the Father, is the sovereign of faith.

Jesus Christ is the supremacy of faith,

For the Holy Spirit is the substance of faith.

Mercy and grace are the covenants of faith.

Where is your faith? And who is your hope?

For the pure in heart are favored after God's own heart

All in all, thy faith witnesses unto God through the Holy Ghost by Jesus Christ.

Vessels of faith are souls of grace;

Holy and whole in the beauty of holiness with binding faith;

Repented faith unto healing faith;

For there is saving faith unto Jesus Christ.

Faith worthiness testifies thy integrity.

God's gift of holy faith made me whole in the image of God.

My soul is whole and my cup runs over in the spirit of faith

Who shall remain full of faith in God's will.

For God's gift of holy faith is freely given in the

Excellency of Holy Ghost power

To the glory of God in perseverance faith.

Faith seeds are revealed, believed and received;

For thy substance of faith sustains thee.

Holy faith has tenacity and integrity.

Hold on to thy faith in Jesus' faith which is God's gift of holy faith. Amen.

Hallelujah

The glory of praise is presence in the spirit of holiness.

Yahweh, Yahweh, Yahweh

Praise psalms, for Yahweh is our God of Glory and his glory gives praise

Unto His name.

Let us sing unto God our songs of praises for

God's gift of praise is thy glory and honor.

For He is our salvation and our God of praise;

Who is our beloved Holy One.

Whose truth glows in the light of His Word by the

Living fire baptism in the spirit of truth.

Hallelujah

His name is worthy above all things,

For there is all praises in the kingdom of God.

Hallelujah

God's children worship in spirit and in truth for our lips

Are covered in praises by the spirit of truth.

For by His truth, God's gift is our praise.

We shall sing praises of song in the glory of God praying in the Holy Ghost.

Hallelujah

Who knows God is praise worthy to worship?

For there is the miracle of light in His glory of praise

Whose light is God's glory.

Hallelujah

There is salvation Sabbath praises in our Lord, Jesus Christ

In the spirit of grace, by our Lord, Jesus Christ.

For the voices of praise shall ring in joy with sanctity.

Praises in the glory of God.

Forever sanctified by grace. My soul and song give praise to God.

There is inspiration into the spiritual joys of hallelujah praise.

Inspired by the Holy Ghost into the soul and spirit.

For my soul is delighted in thy Holy Spirit to be delighted in

Thanksgivings and forgiveness

In thy praise to be delivered and be saved. Hallelujah. Amen.

Holy Anointed Oil

The heavens are opened they pour of anointed rains.

Freedom rains of the Spirit to cleanse my spirit.

Spirit to spirit,

Holy anointed oil is spiritually hallowed unto all true vessels of praise.

Cleanse this vessel Lord to be in thy spirit of truth.

In the unction of the power of the Holy Ghost,

Holy anointed oil rains on me.

Let thy fragrance be perfumed in this vessel of savor.

Pure in heart for Thy glory do I praise Thee.

My heart is free in the spirit of salvation.

For the Spirit of the Holy Ghost anoints the body of the

Church through Jesus Christ,

Who shields the anointed by the holy oil of grace.

For this holy oil is anointed to bring spiritual substances to the gift of God

Who are covered in the spirit of prophetic unction.

When the holy oil is anointed, it is prayed over with

Petitions of love unto the Lord, our God,

Who is the true vine, that this oil shall make contact unto the believer in

Order that he shall receive the

Healings of God and the love in praising worship unto God with reverence.

In grace, this anointed oil preserves the believer in the faith of God.

For the anointed oil truly becomes the sealing substance of the

Crown of glory and the covenant of grace.

The believer is in Jesus Christ's covenant of salvation,

Which seals the anointed believer and sanctifies the

Believer when the believer is in the gospel of salvation.

He then receives the promises of God's Word with expressed

Obedience and faith to believe and to trust our God to serve

Faithfully in the full anointing and blessing by the grace of holiness of the

Holy Spirit.

My Holy Father, My God

I love You, my Lord, Jesus Christ

I seek you in prayer and in fasting faith.

I believe in Your gospel because I love You.

I confess and I repent my sins against You and against my neighbors.

Forgive me Dear Lord. Redeem me. Cleanse me in Your love in

Your will dear Lord.

Thank You, heavenly Father.

I have received Your pure gift of salvation, to be pure in Your heart,

Whole in spirit and true to You.

The Gift of Living Waters

Jesus Christ is the gift of living waters and the gift of the Holy Ghost.

When the vaults and gates of heaven are opened,

Jesus Christ is our Savior.

He is our Anointed Savior who offers life by the

Gift of living waters for everlasting.

The gift of living waters is spiritual living waters for eternal life in our holy

God to never thirst;

Who holds the keys of salvation above the heaven of heavens;

For the Spirit breathes unto the body of living waters of the Holy Spirit to

Ensure the gift of the Spirit.

Hallelujah, Hallelujah, Hallelujah.

Listen and hear the voices of these living waters singing praises and

Worshipping the name

Of our Holy Father God; Renewed by the Spirit to worship through the

Fountain of living waters.

Hallelujah, Hallelujah, Hallelujah.

Who is magnificent and mighty bring forth

Thy living waters of spiritual virtue.

For Jesus Christ is thy living waters of salvation in eternal life.

Heavenly fountains spring forth living waters with mighty strings of flow

From heavenly places in Jesus Christ.

The Water of Waters for the saints are of fruitful waters of

Faithful spiritual life

For the true living word of life is by the living Spirit of the Holy Ghost,

Who is the gift of the living waters to sustain life;

Whose thirst draws thy soul near the living waters washing

By the water of the Word;

To cleanse, to heal and to make whole walking in the

Healing of the living waters.

The Spirit lives in the body of Christ to magnify the Lord,

Our God in the living waters

Who are living vessels of living waters in the beauty of holiness.

Who seek the spirit of truth praying in the Holy Ghost by

Jesus Christ's gift of Living Waters.

The Ministry of the Holy Ghost

The ministry of the Holy Ghost is in God's power and authority

For The Holy Ghost quickens the spirit of the Word,

Who is the sanctifier of the soul and the spirit of life,

And He prepares the heart to be sanctified unto

Purification and glorification.

Therefore, Jesus Christ is our Savior and Bishop of our soul,

Who sends the Holy Spirit unto us to witness of our Savior, Jesus Christ,

Who prepares the saints in the ministries of holiness by faithfulness.

There is glory in thy holy name Yahweh

And there is perfection in the beauties of holiness.

The satisfaction of thy soul comes in completion by

Jesus Christ's perfection.

Jesus answers thy soul for redemption, reconciliation, and resurrection

Jesus is the answer to your soul in repentance, forgiveness

Justification to the gift of salvation

In the name of Jesus Christ, the spirit of holiness glorifies grace and mercy.

The Holy Ghost is He who quickens

Thy saints to bear witness in spiritual truths.

The holy fire of the Holy Ghost is God's eternal flames of ministry.

God, the Father, is the sovereignty

Jesus Christ the Son is the supremacy

The Holy Spirit of the Holy Ghost is the power and the authority.

In obedience and faith, the Holy Spirit ministers unto your spirit.

The circumcision of heart is the inspiration of the Holy Spirit

Who calls you to testify in the fellowship of praise.

Listen faithfully while the Holy Ghost ministers unto your spirit.

For Jesus' peace is the ministry of the Holy Spirit and the

Gospel of our salvation.

The Holy Kiss of the Holy Ghost

The Holy Ghost kisses in the purity of holiness,

Who is the sanctifier of holiness

And who is the sealer of the holy covenant.

For the Holy Spirit quickens in the Spirit of the living God who is clothed in

The light of glory by God's holiness, For God's breath is holy.

Whose Holy breath breathes and seals life unto salvation.

For salvation is through the seed of righteousness by our

Lord and Savior Jesus Christ.

For the Holy Ghost comes and covers in the spirit of righteousness

And in the spirit of liberty for grace to grace.

Blessed is the name of our Holy Father.

For the glory of the Holy Ghost faithfully speaks in the spirit of truth,

Who is perfecting the flaming ministries of the Word of God.

For the perfection of holiness is in the Spirit of the Living God.

The Holy Ghost's holy kiss is fulfilled, for there is the sanctity of holiness.

For the Holy Ghost gives favor by the holy kiss of grace and mercy.

Who sanctifies and magnifies the love of God.

For the Holy Ghost is the sanctifier of holiness.

For the kiss of life is who I breathe.

To give glory to our Holy Father is to worship God

In praise and prayer by spirit and truth.

By the faith of Jesus Christ whose kiss breathes salvation for eternity.

For the Holy living kiss of the Holy Ghost lives in the children of God.

Spirit to spirit who are the saints of glory by the holy kiss of the

Holy Ghost. Amen.

The Holy Resurrection of Glory

Jesus Christ is the holy light through the light of glory.

Thy radiance of grace is the glory above glory in the labor of love.

When the Holy Spirit anoints,

The spirit blossoms through the fruit of the Spirit.

Jesus Christ is the holy resurrection of glory and

He is our Passover Lamb of God.

Jesus says, "I am the Resurrection".

For Jesus' ministry is the gift of healings and

Reconciliation unto our Holy Father God

In the spirit of revelation and lightening grace,

Jesus is the glory of radiance.

Where the promise is revealed, there is power, peace and love.

Truly, the glory of radiance glows and flows through the

Authority of the Holy Spirit

For heaven is crowned by the presence of God.

For God's light is magnified and glorified through our Lord, Jesus Christ.

We worshiped God in prayer from repentance to purification and

Sanctification unto glorification.

Immediately, praying in the Holy Ghost in the
Spirit of joy, forgiveness and good will.
Behold, in the kingdom of God, the angel of God
Appears in the spirit of quickness.
The angel of light worships and obeys God and the pure in heart
Opens the gates of heaven in prayer.
Beloved elect chosen saints who are clothed in God's glory
And are cleansed by the blood of Jesus.
As the morning rose,
The angel of God ascends from the earth to the heaven
And from the heaven to the earth,
Just as Jesus Christ rose in the spirit of resurrection by the power and
Authority of the Holy Ghost.
The living Word of God lives from repentance to redemption and
Reconciliation to resurrection
Restored through the Word of God and renewed in the right
Spirit of the Holy Ghost.
God's holy resurrection of glory who have blessed
Thy kingdom heirs of salvation,
From edification and sanctification to justification and to glorification.
We worship with thanksgivings and praises in the Spirit of Truth. Amen.

Grace's Covenant

In the law of faith,

The kingdom of God is here. Judgment rings majesty.

Repentance comes by faith in the newness of life.

Grace ministers mercy.

Grace's covenant of faith, by the justification of grace,

Is for the love of God.

For we know the gift by grace is our free gift,

For the righteousness of faith is justified;

Justified by grace and faith unto redemption.

God anointed Jesus Christ by the Holy Ghost

By whom He is our gift of salvation who reigns through grace.

Through Jesus' faith our atonement from sin and death

Who is our eternal life.

Grace's covenant. Amen.

God's Heart is Near

There is a place where souls are healed and spirits are summoned;

Where souls are saved in the kingdom of God.

There is a place of glorification and justification of love in holy faith

In the kingdom of God.

There is a place of sanctification in the love of Jesus Christ,

Our Savior and Bishop of our souls

By God our Holy Father

Who sealed in His Holy Spirit in heavenly places in

Jesus Christ for His gift of salvation,

Anointed after His Holy Spirit.

This place is where your heart remains

In God's glory by His honor;

Joy, mercy and grace

After God's own heart. Amen.

God is Our Lord

We come to God now. Repented from our sin.

Giving God praise.

We love You Lord, our God.

In the Spirit of God, we worship you Lord. Praying in thy Holy Ghost.

Spirit to spirit in truth.

Glory to glory.

In praise and worship, we are calling Thy holy name.

Jesus is our Lord.

Hallelujah

God is our love of grace.

We bless You, Lord.

In holiness and thanksgiving grace, thank You God for healing me whole.

In love, we thank You God, our Lord.

We bless You Lord in spirit and soul. Amen.

Gifted Children

Gifted children are in the power of God.

The flow of gifted seeds.

Inspired from God's knowledge of love.

Generations to generations

Rich in noble heritage through love.

Gifted children

Spring forth from God to the souls of grace in the spirit of liberty.

Through the love of marriages or hate and rape,

God's Spirit anoints and ordains.

To sanctify these gifted children is to glorify them in the baptism of the

Holy Ghost.

Blessed are the gifted children of grace.

Their voices ring in one accord to the melody of love.

Their passage through time and grace shall be appointed to give

God the glory.

Stars of heaven yield to the children's glory.

They are stars at flow as they glow in the glory of sanctity.

Stars never lost for they are fruitful and truthful.

Gifted seeds

Children glowing

Gifted stars at flow

Gifted children. Children.

God's Children. Amen

Holy

Grace and mercy unto Thee, O Lord,

In Thy fullness and richness of Thy glory. Holy Spirit, hear O Lord.

Who are thy grace to mercy?

For your Word faithfully honors grace and mercy

In truth and spiritual love

For grace is inseparable from mercy. Dear Lord!

What does grace say to mercy?

Then divine words of grace speak spirit filled in truth and trust

Mercy compassionately hears grace as grace ministers unto mercy

Merciful Father, our God.

Jesus says, I am grace in liberty

Who my Father's mercy answers.

The spirit of grace seals my covenant of faith in a

Comely manner of joy and peace

Through the fruits of the Spirit.

These are my testimonies acceptable and pleasing unto the

Father of glory.

I, grace, implore favor in prayer and fasting faith to

Redeem my beloved soul.

I am the bishop of these for the healings in the righteousness of
Jesus Christ
Through the dispensation of grace and mercy in judgment and salvation.
Amen.

Justice

Yahweh, our God ordains and ministers justice.

God's Word is the living oracle to justice.

God, our Holy Father, who is just;

Who seeks justice; for justice is the fruit of judgment.

Jesus is justice. He is holy and meek.

Jesus says, I am justice, I am the Way, the Light and the Truth.

I am the resurrection of justice to do the will of the Father.

True justice lives in salvation.

To know justice and judgment is to know mercy and grace.

Blessed our Savior unto salvation in the ministry of justice

By God's covenant of Grace through the righteousness of God in Jesus

Christ our Bishop and Savior

Of our soul. Who is justice?

For justice is our hope; Justice speaks in the spirit of faith.

In the ministry of God, hear justice's voice who rings faithful in

Truth and spirit.

Prayers and praises word in faith through His laws, commandments,

Statues, precepts, ordinances, judgments and testimonies.

To keep God's testimonies is to keep God's blessings in truth and spirit.

God, who is just, is the Holy One who judges and He is the judge.

He is the faithful one who rules and reigns.

Hallelujah

The Holy Ghost has the power to heal and renew the spirit and the body.

The Word of God washes and regenerates

For we are justified by faith through the grace of Jesus Christ.

God the Father is our sovereignty of justice.

God the Son Jesus Christ is our supremacy of justice.

God's Holy Spirit of Ministries Worship

God's Holy Spirit of ministries worship is ordained by faith.

To know God is to worship God in holiness.

For God's children are in the knowledge of their God.

They worship God in spirit and truth praying in God's Holy Spirit.

Spirit to spirit and faith to faith we worship and serve God.

Through repentance, and redemption, our spirit is renewed and restored.

We are reconciled unto our Holy Father through Jesus Christ.

For the kingdom of glory is glorified by the Holy Ghost.

To know God is to worship God with the fullness of faith being pure and True in heart.

To worship God is to give God His honor in the fear of the Lord.

For God's children have the greatest adoration of love for God's Worthiness and holiness.

We worship God for his supremacy. God is the Son who is Jesus Christ our Lord and Savior and who is

Bishop and Shepherd of our soul who is worthy to be praised.

We worship God for His authority, for God is the Holy Ghost of the Holy Spirit.

Our reverence to God is inspired and revealed in God's Spirit by His Word.

To know God is to worship God faithfully in obedience,

For God's presence is near and He is holy and anointed by the
Power of the Holy Ghost.
For the Holy Father, the Holy Spirit and the Son, Jesus Christ are one.
For there is only one God. For "I am Holy" says the Lord, our God.
I am holy and the children of God commune in Me through prayer.
To worship God in prayer, there is sanctity in the power of God to
Commune with you.
For God is worthy. Worthy is the Lamb.

For the Lamb of God is holy whom we give our homage to by testifying
And confession truth.
In the kingdom of God, the gift of salvation is by God's mercy and grace for
The children of God.
There, in Jesus' heavenly bodies, the children of God worship and praise
God in ministries spirit;
For God's Holy Spirit in ministries spirit blessing
God always in spirit and truth. Amen

God the Holy Ghost is our Authority of Justice

There is all in one and one for all. We are in the body of
Jesus Christ by the Spirit of the Holy Ghost
In heavenly places through the creed and decree of holiness.
Mercier, the beauty of holiness is the beauty of love.
God's love is holiness.
Fully whole and complete in the perfection of holiness
To know the glory of God is to praise and worship God in sprit and truth.
Thy soul speaks and seeks God to praise God first at all times.
Thy soul is pleased to worship and praise God;
God of life, God of Israel, eternal God.
Justice answers judgment.
The law of justice is by the law of faith in love.
In the kingdom of God, all are delivered unto justice.
All are delivered unto justice in the kingdom of God by the wisdom of God,
For the issue of justice measures the sentence of faith and
The sentence of death.
Who shall believe will have life through repentance,
Forgiveness and redemption,
Sanctification, and justification to do justice in the will of God.
Who knows the heart's intent is He who judges the heart.
Who shall do justice and judgment through the power of the

Holy Ghost and through the sanctification of truth by mercy and
Justification of the Spirit by grace in the body of Jesus Christ.
The spirit of justice rests in the spirit of wisdom by the
Sovereignty of the Lord, our God, Jesus Christ.
Through his supremacy of knowledge and understanding by the
Spirit of counsel
Though the power of the Holy Ghost for the heirs of salvation.
Who are you? We are God's children and heirs of salvation;
For God is love, fair and righteous to give justice and
To give life by the gift of salvation

In the authority and the legitimacy of the Holy Spirit
Holding on to the tenacity of truth in the spirit of truth and
Trusting in His mercy and grace.
There must be judgment and justice for the perfection of
Grace and mercy in the faith of God,
For grace justifies mercy to sanctify judgment and
Justice and judgment justifies by justice;
For they are the fruit and habitation of God's throne.
There is power in justice for God's glory.
This power honors his word and his testimony having
True intimacy and legitimacy with God,
For we are truly called the children of God in the Kingdom of God.

By him therefore is our just Savior and Judge who glorifies in

Just righteousness and peace of Jesus Christ.

The Prince of Peace who is justice.

Justice in Jesus Christ our Savior and Bishop of our soul.

Amen.

God's Holy Love

I am holy; the holy being of thy glory.

I am that I am.

I am love.

I am the kingdom of God in thy glory.

Who is holy in love.

I am from love, to love, of love, by love, through love, to love, in love.

In the kingdom of God, I am the preeminence of love in the Holy Ghost.

God is love.

To know love is to know God.

I am the authority, the sovereignty, and supremacy of holy love.

In the kingdom of God, God glorifies and sanctifies love in thy holiness.

God justifies and fortifies love in thy loveliness and righteousness

Through our lord, Jesus Christ.

The gift of holy love is the beauty of holiness.

In the anointing grace of the Holy Spirit, I pray God places the

Seed of love in my heart.

There the seed of love unfolds unto the flower of joy and passion by the

Fruits of the Spirit.

May God cleanse and circumcise my heart in His holy grace of godliness.

In the kingdom of God, love is there and here to worship God holy and Pure in the spirit of truth.

In the fear of the Lord, love requires my heart to seek God first in the Kingdom of God.

In the kingdom of God, love is the sum of all excellence and grace in the Glory of God;

For love esteems and ministers fervently and zealously the law of love.

For in the mercies of love, where love relieves thy soul and God forgives thy sins.

For the substance of love is sprit and truth for love covers sin.

In faith, God's holy love is there and here when you are near in prayer.

God's love is near in the presence of the Holy Ghost.

In the spirit of liberty, love holds and frees unto the holy salvation of glory.

God's love strengthens me in the virtue of worship and honor to trust, Believe, and obey Him only.

In the fear of God, my reverence to God is by the integrity of the Spirit through the obedience of love, mercy, and grace.

God's tender passions of affections and adorations are exceedingly in Kindness for thy beloved.

Love testifies God is holy and true.

I am love. I am holy love.

I am that I am God is holy love. Amen.

I, Too, Feel the Colours of the Wind

For Satan knows every wind and doctrine contrary to God.

He is the father of lies; and he is the liar.

The tempter blows his spiritual winds into the world to attack, to destroy,

To steal, and to kill.

For Jesus Christ knows his children are here to win to the end.

We are God's friends to the end by God's Word of Truth.

But we are tested by the Prince of the Air through the sin of disobedience.

For the wind comes light and bright against me, my God.

I too, know the Spirit of God. Yet, we walk by faith and not by sight.

The Prince of the Air comes and blows sin and death, but the glory of God

Gives righteousness and life,

For Jesus Christ is the glory of the gospel in word and deed.

Must we fight to be right in the spirit of truth and the spirit of liberty?

For Jesus Christ is our righteousness of God through the grace of faith.

Where Satan's wind blows with great might and blight,

God is our safeguard.

Tonight, these dark shadows pass over me to steal, to kill and

To destroy my soul.

I, too, feel the colours of the wind so furiously and angrily.

These tempted winds blow angrily to up root the earth's foundation and
The spirit of my soul.
The Spirit of Christ shall save my soul beyond the fright of the night.
Satan's winds run from the Spirit of God, our crown of glory.
The tempter's fallen flame fails to ascend above the thorn of God.
So his wind goes to and forth, and in and out, up and above and down and
Below where you are.
These winds are full of death, fear, evil and sin of rebellion and deception
Whose spirituality and integrity have been tested by the
Wind and fire of death.
For the wind comes with its power of fear and the
Spirit of disobedience and deception.
To resist the wind is to stand for God's covenant truth, and be verified.
In the Holy Spirit, I now glow in the flow of the light of God to spiritually
Overcome sensuality and fear.
Thanks to Jesus' anointing who overcomes the winds of the tempter.
Peace be still for the winds are ceased and Salvation is blessed
Unto the faithful servant. Amen.

Spirit of Intercession

In the spirit of intercession,

The Holy Ghost bears all things and makes intercession for our souls.

God is our Savior and our salvation.

The voice of God proceeds in the power of the creative word of life.

From the foundation of His Word, all good things were established by His power of authority.

All first fruits yield their kind to give glory to God in Their praises and worship.

The altar of God's sanctuary is sanctified by His love, grace, and mercy.

Through Jesus Christ's preeminence of dominion power,

God's sovereignty, supremacy and the authority of the Holy Ghost comes together to sanctify the word of creation by the living Spirit of God.

Conception.

The Holy Spirit nourishes and refreshes life with the quicken spirit.

In the spirit of Jesus Christ, intercessions are covered for every soul;

For He is our Savior and Bishop of our souls.

There the saints of God have deliverance unto Jesus' peace.

Perception.

The Holy Ghost perceives and reveals spiritual understanding

To walk in the path of God with the right heart.

In the knowledge of God, who keeps you from sinning and falling.

Being in the presence of God's loving grace forgiveness cleans thy soul.

Reception

God prepares the heart to receive His love.

Giving hope and looking for the mercy of our lord, Jesus Christ.

Unto eternal life and honor for the gospel.

Exception.

You must be born again by water and spirit.

Perception.

Remember God's words, precept, commandments

And the doctrine of the gospel of Jesus Christ.

Our legitimacy of grace.

Misconception.

They who separate themselves sensual having not the spirit.

Susception.

Evil is found in sin's pride and sensual lust, doubt, unbelief,

Gear, contempt of the proud where no counsel is the people fall.

Deception.

Disinformation, lies and falsehood, destruction and death are

Satan's fruits.

Judgment is executed for all ungodly deeds and words

Against our holy father, God.

This is their reward and punishment.

Acceptance.

Expressed through your belief in Jesus' faith.

The gospel is true.

The prophesy and the prophets give testimony of Jesus Christ.

Jesus comes and consents admission by true belief in God.

His holy father, God.

Amen.

Tears of My Overflow

God's grace holds my face composure as anointing tears come over me.

The compassion of the Holy Ghost welcomes me in his Spirit.

His spirit is in my heart with anointing grace.

These tears of my overflow are my joy in mercy over justice and judgment.

Tears dwell fountain springs forth from deep wells.

Where my eyes have never seen, the vision of the

Spirit reveals my direction.

In the Spirit of God, anointed eyes see the vision of truth.

Tears of my overflow spiritually understand my fate by my faith.

Why love remembers me today?

God knows where I have been and what I have done in sin.

My tears thank you our God of grace.

In the eyes of God, there is a place near my face where grace covers me.

My tears cover my face and God cleanses my eyes.

Tears of my overflow in the light of Christ

Give prayer from my sinner's path.

Repented tears run over.

Why? Love met me in my needs and have covered

My unanswered prayers.

By the Word of God, God hears my cry over my judgment.

As I hear His soft spoken word, you are forgiven my child.

Tears of my overflow emerge as springs of true love.

You are delivered my child. I have carried you over by my grace.

Soul filled with the joy of love come tears of my overflow

For the glory of God.

For the glory of God, He has worked all things out.

Now, living tender days of love over my troubled heart.

Tears of my over flow have healed all pains.

The Seasons of Love

Thy summer love who fervently increases yet calms and soothes.

In the spring, the living waters of Jesus Christ lift my soul

And in the fall, grace comforts me in the Holy Spirit.

I am here in salvation. I am saved by faith.

In the winter's blissed, love is warmhearted to melt joy and peace deep in my soul.

To know love is to know God.

Thy benevolent voice calls the Lord.

In the fear of the Lord, I hear from thy Spirit to my heart.

In the melody of godliness, loveliness and holiness,

I hear the voice of God so sweet and good.

I am here in salvation.

In faith, I am saved in the seasons of love. Amen.

Salvation is God's Gift to the Church

O God, my hope unto eternal life is thy promise.

God is salvation.

Thou God of my salvation who is my hope unto eternal life,

Deliver me from sin.

You are thy power, honor, and glory.

Jesus Christ is my hope and the promised gospel of salvation.

Thy anointed prayers and communion are in faith.

This salvation comes unto you through Christ our Lord and Savior,

Who is thy light and joy.

Salvation is our gift of grace;

Sanctifying the spirit of love by the body of Christ.

For salvation is God's gift to the church.

In grace and mercy, the Holy Spirit sanctifies thy soul.

To sanctify God's glory is to love God in the communion of the Holy Spirit.

Thy peace is in the unity of truth. Who is thy author of salvation?

Thou God of my salvation is true. Amen.

The Anointed Touch

For the children of God, there are the blessings of the anointed touch.

There are many souls who have the need of God's healing touch.

Here am I Lord, my God, I need Your anointed touch in my life.

To know the touch of God is to know the sanctity of love.

There is the woman of God and the man of God before me.

Their prayers of grace are faithfully prayed.

My soul rejoices to know saints of God have prayed for me.

Suddenly, as I walked the faith walk to the altar of grace,

I know the anointed touch of God is present.

As the Holy Spirit moves suddenly,

I have received the anointing touch of the Holy Ghost. Amen.

I thank You, Holy Father, because I believe in

Your ministry of the Holy Ghost;

For thy holy presence is near unto my soul. My soul praises Thee.

My soul yields unto God's presence with a pure heart of love and joy.

As the anointed touch of God is given,

I am so relieved and blessed to believe in God's holy calling.

By the gift of the anointed touch, God's hand of grace and mercy is upon

Me in His name of glory.

In the glory of the gospel, Jesus Christ is the crown of glory who blesses my Soul in the authority of God.

When I looked up, the holiness and loveliness of grace has covered the Crown of my head.

My heart and face shine in the glory of God with awesome delight.

Immediately, the light of glory opens my heart in God's word;

For God's word governs over me in spirit from my heart to my soul;

For God prepares my heart and my mouth in what to know and say.

I am anointed and comforted by the grace of Jesus Christ's anointed touch through the Holy Ghost.

I am thankful to be forgiven of my sin and I am healed and delivered in Jesus' righteousness of peace.

Now, I seek the kingdom of God in the Meekness of prayer in the spirit of truth.

Surely, the power of love is the gift of God in God's anointed touch;

For the gift of God is freely given by His grace. Amen.

Sin's Season

In the image of Satan, there is spiritual sin.

Sin is only a false pleasure for a season.

Sin is of the spirit of instability.

In the spirit of lust, there are seducing spirits, contrary spirits and Controlling spirits;

For the season of sin comes and goes through the airs of lust and lies.

In the influence of sin, to seduce by temptation,

To destroy and to kill thy soul to devour it for eternal death.

This fury is fuel for hell's judgment,

For God hates sin and sentences Satan forever in judgement.

Satan is the father of confusion who hides in the spirit of imperfection.

Faithless in the glory of false worship in lies and death.

Satan coerces worship for the kingdom of death.

Who is subverting and coverting over the poor and lost in the Spirit of disobedience.

From the north gate to the south gate,

He looks to prey on the innocent souls.

To the east gate to the west gate, he preys in waiting and watching the

Clues to tempt, to destroy, to defile, to degrade,

To demoralize and kill thy soul.

Satan's fruits are evil attributes in the spirit of adultery, anxious,

Blasphemy, breaches of trust, covenant breakers, covetousness,

Drunkenness, emulation, hypocrisy and drunkenness, cruelty, deceit,

Delusion, depression, discouragement, dishonesty, disobedience,

Distraction, envy, evil eye, evil thoughts, foolishness, fornication,

False witness, greed, guilt, hatred, haughty eyes, heresies, hallucination,

Idolatry, Laziness, lasciviousness, murder, obsession, pride, resentful,

Reviling, secret, worry, stagnation, fraud, depravity, corruption,

Captivated arts, shame, shedding innocent blood,

Theft and denying the truth.

Who is the antichrist?

The accuser and the oppressor of evil possession, who is Satan.

The culprit in the pulpit is the antichrist sin's season for the pleasure of sin.
Amen.

The Eye of Pride

Behold, the eye of pride sees from the lust of the flesh and
The lust of the heart.
Who loves to have the preeminence over souls and spirits.
There is no fear of the Lord in the eye of pride,
For God hates the evil in the eye of pride.
Christ is He who has the preeminence.
Thy soul testifies thy wicked heart of deceitfulness.
Christ is He who knows thy heart and thy fruits.
Thy countenance appears through the Prince of the Air;
Who is the father of lies, evil, sin and destruction. Face to face.
Thy countenance bears wicked imaginations and false witnessing.

In thy spirit of contention and adversity,
There is enmity, vanity and apostasy.
Discord crowns pride in self praise.
Whose proud look bears thy countenance of pride and a prideful spirit.
Who examines thy self and appraises one's self above all others with
Arrogance and a haughty heart.
Pride speaks to the mind and spirit as sin is never satisfied,
Nor is the eye of pride in sin.
Pride seeks to destroy souls by measure of sight and vision.

Thy spirit bears witness and thy fruit is revealed.

Thy eye of pride sees thy estimation above the throne of God.

Deceived by self-esteem, self-admonition, self-reliance, and self-will.
Through the scope of dishonesty and disunity,
Thy visions are perverted in judgment.
Who is deceived by the appearance of truth in falsehood
Through the eye of the storm, the crisis, the test is revealed.
A prince of lies, who is a liar of sensuality and
Walks with the appearance of virtue
As opened eyes as gods of the flesh in lust of the world
And the pride of knowledge.
An accuser who accused the innocence.
Who charges the victim with fault by fraud and falsehood,
Who does not admit nor acknowledge thy sin,
Who questions Gods word with doubt.
An evil eye lifted up whose glory is in his pride,
For pride testifies against the truth and the humble with the
Spirit of preeminence and never repent in the eye of pride. Amen.

Christian Suffrage in Spiritual Significance

Jesus' ministry shows an impeccable strength in His suffrage. Ministries for the Christian are firmly rooted in the foundation of Christ. Christ's fulfillment in the law, suffrage of human sin and God's divine wrath have significantly strengthened the spiritual bonds and relationships with man and Christ. This foundation in Christ promotes the Christian to have fundamental accountability in responsiveness to the Christian life. This inevitably establishes accountability and responsibility to the nature of Christian grace and mercy to maintain a holy attitude, behavior and responsiveness in social relationships. The Christian begins this profile in character to proclaim obedience in faith unto our holy Father God, our Lord.

Dear Lord our God, since the Christians are charged with this covenant of fiduciary principles in duties, responsiveness to the circumcised heart of a spiritual nature in the same mind as Christ.

Suffering is declared upon the Christian believers to be tested in their Christian demeanor and mannerism in character. Jesus expressed these fundamental values which are indeed deemed in a Christian's love, mannerism and trust in their faith of Jesus Christ. These values are held dear for Christ in the suffering for the sake of righteousness in Christ Jesus which is considerable in honor and acceptability to our Lord God and Savior, Jesus Christ (1 Pet. 2:20, 1 Pet. 3:14-17).

Christians are definitely no better than Christ in their suffering. Especially, "For our Lord has suffered great pains enduring the event of the false trial held, the cross, the physical pain of flesh piercing abuse by whipped torn flesh in terrible wounds and stakes driven through His hands as He hung on the cross (John 19:2). Jesus also suffered leadership rejection by not recognizing who He really was but rather chose Caesar for their king. Jesus also suffered mocking, insults, threats, traitorous acts from His beloved and chosen. He suffered injustice being falsely accused for it was mandated that He must suffer for us (1 Pet. 2:20-22). Jesus fulfilled the scripture receiving God's judgement on Him in place of our sins as He was forsaken (Isa. 53:4-5, 1 Pet. 2:24).

The Word of God counsels Christians to think holy in all things in manners of conversation in the same ways as Jesus, because our God is holy. This shows how the Christian's heart must be prepared to respond and to demonstrate proper conduct in governing the gift of faith. The Christian must be led in the way to go. Jesus will instruct you and teach you in the way you should go because He has counseled you with His word and His eye remains upon you, His begotten children (Ps. 32:8).

Christian suffrage is valuable in purifying his soul under obedience unto God, no matter the circumstances, as long as he gives faith in his trust through the spirit of God's love. The spiritual suffrage a Christian goes through is very important and values his spiritual development in relation to God's response to His covenant in deliverance to the Christian obedience in faith, strength, stability and love.

These essential spiritual values are necessary for the Christian to develop a spiritual personality. Therefore, the test of suffrage maintains courage in the Christian in the good faith and spirit of God which will be rewarded in Christ Jesus (Rom. 8:12-18).

The value of responding to suffering as a Christian in a correct manner of conduct says something about the Christian's maturity in Jesus. The Christian is held accountable in responding in godliness. His expressions in manner of speech, action and heart not to grieve the Holy Spirit in any injury, harm, despair and affliction because Jesus has paid the cost and the penalty of death in order that the lost and whomever follow him shall have eternal life in his salvation. Amen.

Spirit of the Word

God is the Word of Life and the Word is the spirit of God.

The Word is God's virtue and eternal testimony.

God's Word remains our covenant of magnificent and majestic Blessings.

In the sanctity of prayer, praise and promise, the word ministers

Preachers, pastors, priests, prophets, hearers and doers.

For God's Word is anointed and ordained by the Holy Ghost.

The voice of the living God speaks His word faithfully.

Wherein, the Holy Ghost powers thy counsel in the stillness of speech;

God the Father, God the Son, God the Holy Ghost.

There is power in the spirit of the Word.

To perceive, to believe, and to receive

God's gift is to be in the spirit of the Word.

In the spirit of grace, Jesus ministers mercy,

There is faith in the living Word;

The prophetic word, the spoken word, the written word,

And the revealed word.

Jesus speaks the prophecy, the Holy Scriptures,

The spirit of the word revealed.

God's Word carries volumes of truths in the spirit.

The Comforter is near to relieve your soul.
Be not deceived nor grieved.
How can you see and hear and not perceive?
The Spirit commands the phonology of the word to heal,
To create, to live and to love our
Soul against sin.
The word of the Lord speaks thy safeguards as a mighty sword
To those who obey and hear God's Word with the
Fear of the Lord is to them
The beginning of knowledge, wisdom and
Understanding in spiritual discernment.
In the unity of the spirit, the kingdom of God
Comes in the spirit of the Word.
The spirit of the Word is the oracle of the law of grace.
In prayer, the Word shields and nourishes thy soul.
In praise, the glory of God is unto us His gift of salvation;
For God is who our soul loves.
In faith, His word answers above the nights and the days of heaven.
God's Word answers in the Godhead of the supremacy,
Authority, sovereignty, who enlightens, defends
And calls the children of God.
The spirit of the Word is the sanctity of truth, the stability of peace and

The beauty of Holiness in the kingdom of God.
The Lord sings prayers and the holy oracles in
Thanksgivings and forgiveness.
The Word of God voices commandments,
Testimonies, precepts, ordinance,
Statutes, laws, principles, orders, decrees, rules,
Instructions, justice and judgments.
The Word of God springs forth great fountains of living waters to wash
Our souls in truth.
The Word is He who is the seed of life in all seasons.
For the word discerns the heart in all things
According to truth in the faith of God.
The word of the Lord speaks to your soul in spirit and truth;
Who calls you by name and has a place for your soul
For your words and deeds.
Jesus is our Savior and Bishop of our souls
In the kingdom of God by the spirit of the Word.
Jesus is the spirit of the Word. The word of sovereignty,
Supremacy, and authority
All power is inherent unto Christ our Lord and Savior
By the spirit of the Word of God and witnessed by the Holy Ghost.
Amen.

The Mother of Life

The mother of life is called to be in God's trust,
For the children of life are God's gift to praise.
Sweet womb of liberty is for her promised child.
The gift of life springs forth and answers in the grace of God.
She spiritually discerns and enlightens her child.
She praises God for the beloved mother who she is blessed to be.
Her spirit bears witness to the faithful testimonies of God's will.
The blood of life bears witness to all generations;
Mother to mother and child to child.
The seed of life of the mother's law begins in the spirit of liberty,
For she is honored for her motherhood,
Who is thy mother of life in the will of God;
For the mother of life safeguards from fears and shields from danger.
Her voice is heard unto the unborn child as
She carries the promised child.
Commissioned to carry the call of freedom in the
Liberty of spirit is the life of the spirit.
Her melody sings comfort and peace for the mercy of God.
In the home, a mother's heart speaks the prayers of life unto her
Promised child.
Here is a mother's heart with a sweet, tender touch of the

Spirit of trust in God's faith.
The mother's love nourishes thy soul in spirit and truth in the
Word of God.
The mother's milk nourishes thy soul by the message of God in strength
And courage,
For the law of thy mother is sealed of her heart
In the covenant of grace.
A mother's kiss seals hope as every day unfolds.
Her kiss covers and sanctifies the body of her infant
From new life in the kingdom of God.
From thy tender toes unto the crown of thy head, she is covered.
The mother's voice cries out in prayers and joys for
Protection and direction of her
Child's soul unto the Lord, our God.
In the law of thy mother, her head crowns the purposes of the will of
God to be my faith.
Thy mother's neck towers in the balances of understanding and the
Knowledge of the wisdom of God.
Every mother has the love of God upon her heart, for her arms softly
Comfort me upon her bosom of life.
Thy mother is a woman of God in ministries spirit.
Her hand gently smooths the way of any harm for the

Word of God is the way.

Thy mother's eyes are a watch tower for the sight of glory,

For her ears receive the sounds of my every need in tone and spirit.

The mother of life humbly walks in faith for the joy of the Lord, our God.

For the mother of life is the glory unto God.

Amen.

The Spirit of Hospitality

In the Spirit of Hospitality,
The Holy Ghost greets and welcomes the children of God
Who are pure in heart and dear to the Lord, our God.
God's Holy Spirit ushers in the spirit of hospitality
To seal the hearts of the
Worshipper to praise and to worship Him truly in spirit and truth,
For the heirs of the kingdom of God believe in Him to be relieved
In the spirit of liberty,
For the children of God bear
Witness to great utterance in the spirit of hospitality
And in the spirit of communion.
Faith in Jesus Christ to esteem God's joy in the
Spirit of our Lord and Savior Jesus Christ.
The Holy Spirit is the reception of peace and comfort
In the strength of God;
For the joy of the meek, who loves our beloved
Jesus Christ, esteems Him with adoration;
For Jesus Christ fortifies heavenly places in
His body to worship God in the spirit of hospitality
Which is our prayer of hospitality.
That we are heirs and children of God in the spirit of hospitality.

Yes, Jesus Christ covers our souls in the freedom of grace and in the
Spirit of Liberty praying in the Holy Ghost
And in hospitality ministry.
The gift of the Holy Ghost sanctifies our souls in the
Holy Spirit and in the spirit of truth.
In the kingdom of God, there is spiritual significance in the
Spirit of truth;
For the reception of membership, companionship,
Fellowship and friendship
For the relationship in God, our Holy Father.
Who are esteeming one another greater than ourselves in
Faith through our Lord and Savior Jesus Christ,
For He is the Bishop of our souls;
Who testifies in the spirit of hospitality to prepare the
Hearts of the saints to
Receive the grateful reception in the spirit of hospitality.
Jesus Christ is our Messiah; Who is the anointed Savior;
Who is ordained in the might, power and strength of the Holy Ghost.
Holiness and hospitality come to glorify
God's presence in the will of God.
In hospitality ministry, the kingdom of God reveals
The grace of the church.

This salutation of hospitality gives legitimacy and
Intimacy to the love of Christ.
In the beauty of holiness, the saints gather themselves in
Fellowship to give God the glorification in unification
In one faith and one body.
This reception shows that we are honored and we are valued.
There is hope, peace and love in the gift of the spirit of hospitality.
We are welcome again to be in God's presence for eternal life. Amen.

My Soul Praises

My soul praises thy Holy Father.

My soul is thy praise unto Thee. My soul praises my God;

Praises of mercy and grace

Because He lives and He heals and He loves.

My breath of praise breathes His life to follow
His will and to know His grace.
My soul is comely because I praise our Holy Father.
Thank you, Holy Father, to have forgiven
My soul to enable me to praise;
For your righteousness is Jesus Christ.
For You alone are worthy of all praises from
Your creation of the kingdom of heaven
Unto the kingdom of God. Love justifies praise for justice.
My soul is redeemed.
My soul is restored.
My soul uplifts Your presence, Holy Father God.
My soul hungers to praise Your name and Your honor.
My tongue thirsts to taste the joy of your glory.
The will of God is discerned in my soul.

Praise in hope and grace.

My soul is meek in the spirit of love to praise thy Holy Father, God.

Amen.

The Ministry of Miracles

The ministry of miracles is in God's power and authority.
Spiritual miracles are ministered through the yielding spirit,
For the Holy Ghost quickens the spirit of the Word.
God's Word ministers living miracles
And He prepares the heart to be sanctified unto
Purification and glorification.
Therefore, Jesus Christ is our Savior and Bishop of our soul;
Who sends the Holy Spirit unto us to witness of our Savior, Jesus Christ,
Who prepares the saints in the ministries of holiness by faithfulness.
There is glory in thy holy name, Yahweh
And there is perfection in the beauty of holiness.
The satisfaction of thy soul comes in completion by
Jesus Christ's perfection.
Jesus answers thy soul for redemption, reconciliation and resurrection.
Miracles are composed in the kingdom of God.
They are the substance of spiritual fruits and manners
According to their law above laws.
God is our miracle. He is our spiritual and natural miracle,
For life is a miracle and all the kingdoms bare witness unto God.
In miracles, God's marvelous works are shown.
Miracles are done in the glory of God that

We may praise and worship our God.
The birth of a miracle comes now.
Jesus' birth is our miracle to witness to the lost and to witness
Testimonies against the law of sin is Jesus' will of God.
Who knows that sin yields death constantly but,
The witness testimonies of the law of grace are pure
And His grace yields life in the miracle of the spirit,
For God surely overpowers the laws of nature and spirit.
In the glories of holiness, God's acts of judgment and mercy by miracles.
But the eye of the flesh sees a miracle as an unusual thing.
God is the beginning of miracles for miracles manifests the glory of God.
There is nothing too hard for God to do,
Who grants favor in the light of your faith.
Pleasing faith unto God is in the affirmation of miracles for the
Non-believer to believe.
The admiration of faith is witness unto the deaf to hear, the blind to see,
The lepers to be healed, the crippled to be healed and
Thousands fed by miracle food,
Who are now esteemed in faith giving their testimonies.
The wonder power of God is astonishing work of our Creator.
So extraordinary in all good deeds, for God's dealings with His children
when God decides to do miracles to show miracles for correction

And chastening for His glory.

The kingdom of glory.

For faith is manifested in the pure heart for the things of a miracle.

They are done in word and deed by the Spirit through true faithfulness.

Why water turned into wine? Or raising death into life?

Suddenly, Jesus is our resurrection.

The issue of blood is healed. Walk on the water in the word.

To whom needs the miracle of Jesus is to him

Who asks to be healed in faith.

Amen.

God's Glorified Virtue

God glorifies in thy virtue to cover us in comfort by
His anointed power and authority of the Holy Ghost.
God's spiritual powers are in the power of prayer,
For God's glorified virtue is magnified in mighty strength of the
Holy Spirit.
He is my Comforter and the keeper of my soul through the holy Word,
For the Word of God is God's gift of strength,
Who is our light from above.
The Spirit of God speaks and declares I am the Lord, your God.
There is power in prayer communion with our Lord and Savior.
The Sabbath rest is God's perpetual strength;
Who is our fortitude and virtue.
Behold, I am God your Holy Father who sustains the kingdom of God by
The first fruit of My strength in **the spirit of truth**
To know God's virtue and valor is to know His glory.
Hallelujah, hallowed be Thy name, for His name is glorified and sanctified.
Thy name is empowered in the holy anointing by the
Authority of the Holy Ghost,
Who is the glory of thy power and strength.
Thy hand is thy healing balm of grace.

Thy arm is thy strength of mercy and grace.
In His Word, the voice of thunder speaks and the
Sword of lightning strikes.
Jesus breathes through the air of the winds to seal the kingdom of God.
Jesus is the head and supremacy of the power of strength and authority.
The Godhead is the power of thy sovereignty, supremacy
And authority in the Holy Ghost.
The sacred holy Word of God is thy strength of thy Spirit
Who is ordained and anointed mightily in the strength of truth and spirit.
Who is consecrated in the wisdom of God by faith.
Jesus Christ is the power of the gospel, who is the power of glory and the
Glory of holiness, who reigns in power of salvation.
Who illuminates in God's glory, for the light of glory is
Thy strength to fulfill all promises.
Thy resurrection virtue is thy strength and virtue.
Thy oracles of strength are thy Word.
For the Lord, thy God, is the strength of truth
And thy shield and thy sword of the Word.
The seal of God is the seed of the Word, who is the giver of life,
For God's spiritual sovereignty rests in His Sabbath
Through the supremacy of our Lord Jesus Christ and the authority of the
Holy Spirit.

Behold God's strength never ceases in the spirit of love and
The beauty of holiness,
For the glory of God is Thy spiritual seed of the Word.
Thy virtue and valor from glory to glory.
Who are filled by the overflows of His Spirit.
His dominion reigns over all kingdoms.
In spiritual worship, there is power in the strength of God.
There is power to hallow Thy name in Thy sacred anointing.
In Jesus, there is power to lay down His life and power to lift up His life.
There is power to heal and to keep safe.
There is power to never die and to never lie.
There is power to write your name in heavenly places in the
Sealed books of God. There is power to fear the Lord, thy God.
There is power to hold and to keep, to save and to deliver us
Through our issues of life.
There is power to cast out evil spirits, demons, Satan, sin and death.
There is power to love in the knowledge and understanding and
Wisdom of God.
There is power to express genuine hope, faith and love by the
Word of God.
There is power to sanctify spiritual blessings to follow
Jesus Christ unto eternity.

God Our Holy Father

God, our Holy Father, who is sacred among us? God is holy.
Who gives us His Spirit and breath to breathe?
Blessed be His name.
Who do we call in our inner most secret places?
For His name is holy. Hallowed be thy name, Yahweh, for Thy name is glorified.
From sanctification to glorification
To redemption to salvation in the kingdom of God,
For He is magnified beyond the heavens and the earth
Because He is our true and living God.
Whose sovereign power is the supremacy and the Authority above all things.
Our Holy Father, I pray, to have communion with You.
Renew my prayer with fasting faith believing in You.
Holy Father God, be my portion of faith,
For I have been weakened in sin under Satan's unrighteousness.
Repent my heart with saving faith.
Have mercy, Holy Father. Come in and win my soul.
Please forgive me for my sin.
Let Your heart be near, Holy Father.

I pray, Your Word remain here in my soul with hope.
Please remember to redeem my soul and make me humble and meek.
Perfect Your mercy and grace to allow me to walk by faith.
Let them speak ministry unto my spirit
And prepare my heart according to Your living Word and promises.
Repent, my heart, my God.
Let Thy sword of light open Thy seal of glory
And deliver me to be Your free vessel of mercy
To worship You worthy of thy faith with praises and thanksgiving.
Let us be true to the faith in the spirit and sanctified by the Holy Ghost.
I pray to be the father and husband you have me to be.
Grant my spirit to serve You with a right and clean spirit to welcome
Your Holy Spirit.
I give my children and family to You that You shall bless them
And restore them for Your will and purpose.
Hallelujah, glory and honor.
Our Holy Father; our salvation. Amen.

The Father's Prayer

God prepares and anoints the father by His love,
For the father is summoned to be fruitful and multiply.
Thy father is the principal head to his household.
All honor is given for his valor and virtue.
His daily bread is prepared.
Faith, fortitude, courage and boldness are strengths to his prayers
Unto God, our Holy Father God.
Thy father's blessings
Shall come through his prayers and wise counsel from
God by the Holy Ghost.
He shall have communion and fellowship with
God in their personal relationship
As the same from their fathers of old.
Let every father connect to his children by his spirit, voice, eyes
Heart and hand.
Let him reach his children with his touch of faith.
Let him raise his children up to be great.
Listen, my son and my daughter, while my voice calls your name.
While the blood of life springs up thy fountains through my veins.
I leave you not fatherless for God is our eternal Father.

I shall go to a place to sleep with my fathers
When my destiny is fulfilled.
May my voice resound in you always to correct you and
Discipline you in the way.
We have always nourished your souls as your parents.
We give thanks to God for all His blessings from
Natural foods to spiritual foods.
Remember to always obey us that your soul shall prosper in God's will.
Have a prayerful heart and sanctify the love of our
Father in your hearts, too.
In the light of my Father, his glow shines in the glory of his strength.
How mighty he remains forever in the labor of love.
The strength of my father's arm is always mighty
Trusting only in God's power.
His hands are strong in heart to every touch for deeds of joy.
His eyes blaze with honor and grace to observe the power of light.
When my father put me to bed,
He touched my toes with the blessings of faith.
My faithful father with caring hands and his face
So full of delight in the treasures of his heart.
Let our household of faith be established on
God's Word as we worship Him daily.

Thank You, my heavenly Father,
For my love and my integrity for You by my family.
May I rest in Your holiness and glory of salvation by Jesus' faith.
Amen.

The Prayer of Faith

Faith is the answer to your prayer.
Jesus' faithful anointing inspires the heart.
Who is thy covenant of faith,
For faith is the power of the Holy Ghost.
Our Holy Father God says,
Who I am well-pleased worship in faith, spirit, and truth.
Children of God, where is thy faith?
Whose faith is full?
Is this faith small or great, weak or strong?
Jesus' faithfulness anoints and inspires the heart.
Do you trust in the faith for your prayers?
Holiness assures the promise of salvation healings,
For praying without faith is not of God.
The spirit of fear and doubt are not of God,
For fasting faith in prayer sanctifies truth.
Where is thy faith, children of God?
My faith is filled with the Spirit of God; filled with the knowledge of
God's will In spiritual wisdom and understanding.
What mountains have been moved by faith?
Thy spirit is faithful and fruitful in the blessing of God;

For God knows thy heart and thy fruit of your heart, children of God.

Thy portion of faith is thy virtue and worthiness of your faith.

Let thy tongue confess your faith.

Thy soul cries.

Is your faith walk worthy of God?

Let thy faith be pleasing unto the Lord in prayer

And be faithful in all things of God.

Thy virtue of faith stands in relationship to your communion in Jesus Christ.

Thy faith witnesses Jesus' grace who believes on the name of Jesus.

Glory to glory, grace to grace,

In the prayer of faith. Amen.

Holy Fire of the Holy Ghost

Holy Ghost fire

Baptized by the Holy Ghost

Holy fire of the Holy Ghost

God anoints Jesus in the power of the Holy Ghost

To heal the oppressed, to heal the sick and to raise the dead.

Redemption, reconciliation and resurrection

In the Spirit of the Holy Ghost fire.

Baptism of the fire of the Holy Ghost. Holy Ghost fire.

Jesus walks me through the fire.

The Holy fire of the Holy Ghost.

He lifts me up when I am humble.

He cleanses my vessel unto His will.

Sanctifying a living sacrifice of praise.

The fire of the Holy Spirit directs me with an eternal flame of ministry.

He talks to me through His word by His creation

And He quickens the Holy Ghost's Spirit through the spirit of revelation.

He brings me His eternal peace when I am still in holiness.

I am not alone in the cover of Jesus' glory.

His still quiet voice is faithfully heard.

Praise of obedience and prayer communion to thy ear.

A faithful ear, anointed by the Holy Ghost, for the gift of salvation.

Jesus commands deliverance of faith who delivered my soul.
To be covered and sealed in His glory
Is to be heard in obedience by Jesus' faith.
Reserved in His word and promised salvation
Empowered by God's holy fire of the Holy Ghost.
Holy Ghost fire.
Amen.

God's Wisdom Speaks

Wisdom ye know who knows wisdom? Do you know wisdom?
I know wisdom in God's spirit of wisdom and holiness;
For God, the Father, is the beginning of wisdom. I know wisdom in the fear of the Lord, our God.

I know wisdom
To know all things of Jesus Christ is
To have wisdom in authority, and power of the Holy Ghost.
I know wisdom who is anointed and ordained in God's Holy Spirit praying in the Holy Ghost.
I know wisdom who testifies the truth of God.

Wisdom speaks into thy souls to worship God in spirit and truth.
Wisdom reveals truths which God reveals in the light of truth,
For thy soul knows God whom we praise. Wisdom calls my soul through my heart.
To know our God our heavenly Father is to know His wisdom is faithful and trustworthy.
Wisdom glorifies God's testimonies in truth.
Who is Wisdom? Do ye know wisdom? Whose reception and perception are clearly true.

Whose touch fulfills grace and mercy, kindness and peace.
How sweet is the taste of wisdom,
Discerning the intimacy of spirit and truth.
Who knows the ways of wisdom? Such illumination of mind, when the Spirit bears witness in clarity.
For the power of knowing is knowledge of virtue in the Spirit of God.
Wisdom is knowledge when God's understanding is applied.
I, wisdom, offer prayer in communion of the Holy Spirit and fasting faith.
Who walks by your side, my beloved.
Who counsels thyself in thy obedience of God's will.
Spiritual wisdom is the gift of God.
Who shall receive this gift of wisdom?
God's children ask and it is freely given to worship and to praise God in spirit and truth.
Whosoever is lowly and humble.
For the gift of wisdom is come.
Salvation is the wisdom of God,
For the gift of salvation is yours in the knowledge of God.
This is your gift of life in the kingdom of God,
For God's wisdom speaks.
Amen.

Spirit of Liberty

God is the spirit of liberty.
In the law of liberty, there is liberty in the Spirit of God,
For God's righteousness is in Jesus Christ
Who is our spirit of liberty;
Who is our freedom to worship God in spirit and truth.
Indeed, the spirit of liberty is through our Lord and Savior,
Jesus Christ,
According to God's faithful Word, His will,
His ways and His works.
For Jesus' faith lives by the spirit of liberty
To heal the health of the
Church body in the spirit.
Where there is God's liberty,
There is God's power, authority and legitimacy;
For Jesus' faith is justified, glorified,
Reconciled and perfected.
The life in the virtue of Christ is of the Spirit of God,
The Holy Spirit who is of the Holy Ghost;
For the spirit of liberty crowns thy righteousness by the
Holy Spirit of Jesus Christ.
Thy kingdom of holiness remains by the

Sword of the word.

Thy kingdom is come.

Who comes in the spirit of liberty

For the children of God to proclaim their freedom;

Victory beyond sin, Satan's evil deeds and

Death of the world.

For the kingdom of glory is glorified by the Holy Spirit.

For the kingdom of God is justified by God, our Father.

For the kingdom of heaven is sealed and reconciled by

Our Lord and Savior Jesus Christ.

For grace is the beauties of the spirit

Which is quickened by the spirit of liberty

In God"s holiness.

The Holy Ghost moves in spirit quickness.

There is freedom in the spirit of liberty,

For the spirit of liberty rings faithfully by charity in

Christ's victory.

Ring freedom rings where the spirit of liberty remains,

For the spirit of liberty is the body of Christ.

The children of God are free to do the will of

God in the body of Christ,

For truth is revealed in the spirit of liberty

Who are free to know God"s truth and wisdom.

We are free to obey God's word by

His Holy spirit of liberty.

Amen.

God's Gift of Praise

A prayer of praise, praying in the Holy Ghost
Through Jesus' truth, grace, mercy, peace, and faith
Vessels of honor and salvation through
Jesus Christ our Savior created and endowed
To give testimonies of praises unto the Lord, our God.
Hallowed and ordained
Children of God for their souls to be holy
To exalt Thee, to praise in holiness, to worship God in spirit and truth
According to thy virtue of righteousness in Christ Jesus.
There is obedience of God to give praise unto Him,
To give according to thy portion of grace in love
Is to return all in prayer and praise for my soul lives to praise God.
Praise and prayer is God's communion of faith.
In the image of Christ, who gives us the keys of the kingdom of God.
Unto these hallowed praises, we magnified Him with thanksgiving.
To call upon God with the voice of cheer and gladness
Is to know God is our praise,
Whom I will praise in spiritual virtues in joy, love, peace and faith by
the Grace of wisdom, understanding and
Knowledge in the fear of the Lord.
In the spirit of praise, thy soul by grace lives to glorify God.

My soul loves God.

I delight my soul in Thy glory and light of praises.

You return unto us blessings to praise You without cost,

For we triumph in Thy praise.

The gift of healing for our soul in these praise psalms.

To give God our gift of praise is to give our gift of faith

Wholeheartedly full of praise,

For the voice of praise is of the circumcision of heart.

God's gift of praise. Amen.

The Holy Seed of the Holy Ghost

The holy seed of the Holy Ghost is anointed and glorified.
Who is the living seed of the Holy Ghost?
The seed is the Word in the Spirit of God.
Jesus Christ is the anointed living seed and the word of the Holy Ghost.
Perfection and purification yield the spirit of truth in the power of the
Holy Ghost.
Jesus Christ alone seals the covenant of life through grace for the gift
Of salvation after God's own heart.
Jesus Christ is God's holy gift, who is the God seed of the Godhead.
Immediately, God brings forth His gift in
Jesus Christ with all Godspeed.
Who is faithful and fruitful to magnify our
Holy Father God by His holy name. Yahweh.
Hallelujah, Hallelujah, Hallelujah.
He is the full God seed in the Godhead of grace.
The spirit of Thy Word speaks Holy Ghost power in the
Spirit of liberty for deliverance.
The ready seed in obedience, honor and glory is
He who heals our every need.
Receive the holy seed of Jesus Christ through the
Word in the power of the Holy Ghost,

For the Holy Spirit prepares the heart of circumcision,
For the circumcised heart receives the revelation of the Holy Spirit.
The holy seed is planted in the spirit of the circumcised heart to
Receive God in every need and deed.
The Word of Life is God's seed through the Holy Ghost
Who grows and nourishes our soul in the image of God in prayer by the
Holy Spirit to worship God truly.
In the spirit of grace, Jesus Christ is our priest in the
Sanctification of salvation and the glorification of mercy.
When God's wisdom speaks, it is the fear of the Lord, our God,
Who has come unto us.
Thy seed of holiness speaks unto our soul to worship
God in spirit and in truth.
The seed of the gospel is rightly planted in the children of God
To free and to proclaim the spirit of liberty,
For eternal life is the gift of salvation.
The seed of the Word is by the truth spirit and breath to live eternally.
The seed generates unto the fullness of the generation of man.
By the virtue of the Word, the seed is He who testifies the reverence of
Grace in the beauty of holiness.
In the sanctity of the Word, the seed ministers the proclamation of the
Gospel for the kingdom of God;

For the Holy Ghost anoints and ordains God's seed in the Word of God.
Jesus Christ who is praying in the Holy Ghost that we are heirs of the Kingdom of God.
Who worships God in spirit faithfully, freely and truly.

Through the perfection of the seed of Christ Jesus is He who
Fulfills hope in obedience with trusting belief in
The sovereignty of God is to follow God's will, His word, His ways,
And His works in worship for who God is in
Spirit and truth by the treasures of mercy and grace;
For the seed has the power of the Holy Ghost upon the counsel of God.
Praying, praising and glorifying
God in the beauty of His glories.
Who yields the spirit of the seed and the fruit of the Spirit.
There is authority and power in the Holy Ghost.

There is power in the seed of the Holy Ghost in the spirit of Thy Word,

For Jesus is the seed of the living Word,
Who is loyal and faithful unto truth.
The seed of the written Word of God is revealed
Through the living scriptures.
The seed of the spoken word is the prophetic and the apostolic word.
The seed of the revealed word is the revelation of Jesus Christ from the Holy Ghost.

The seed of the word commands healing and creation in the

Life of the spirit,

For the seed of the Holy Spirit inspires and quickens

The gift of eternal life.

Jesus Christ is the seed of God and the seed of the Word.
The seed is the unity of the spirit and the spirit of the Word.
The Word is He who is the seed of life,
For the Word yields the kingdom of God unto the heirs of the kingdom
Who are the children of God in the promised salvation.
The seed is the oracle of grace who brings us the gospel,
For the seed of the Word seals and shields and nourishes and quickens our

Spirit.

In the sovereignty of God, the supremacy of Jesus Christ and the authority
Of the Holy Ghost, the gospel seeds the word of the Spirit.
For all the legitimacy of the power of the gospel in the
Holy Ghost are inherent in the seed and the word of Truth through our

Lord and Savior Jesus Christ.

The seed is the life fountain within the living waters of the Word
To wash in the spirit and to cleanse our soul in the truth.
Who is the living spirit of the seed and the Word with
God who witnesses and testifies to do the will of
God in the spirit of truth within the holy seed of the Holy Ghost.

God's Holy Passover Prayer

God's holy Passover prayer is for the sanctity of life,

For the spirit of the Holy Ghost prepares and offers the Passover sacrifice.

The miracle of miracles walks the Lamb of God.

Behold, the Lamb of God who is Emmanuel; for God is with us.

The saints of God sing hosanna, hosanna, hosanna

Hosanna is the highest praise.

Hosanna. Blessed is Jesus Christ who comes in the name of the Lord, Our God.

For Jesus Christ is ordained and anointed for the Preparation of the offering.

Worthy is the Lamb of God in the household of faith.

Jesus Christ is our anointed Christ, and the light of love, joy and hope.

Who is our mediator and intercessor for our sin transgression.

For kingdom heirs announce Hosanna to the King,

Jesus Christ in worship and alms.

Blessed this day for our Savior has come.

He comes by the holy gift of the holy fire and the spirit and the water And the blood of Jesus Christ.

For the assembly of the congregation killed the Lamb of God.

For we sing our prayer in remembrance of the Passover Feast and the Feast of Bread.

When God sees the blood of Jesus Christ in judgment and justice and Mercy and grace,

God shall pass over you and judgment will not destroy You as in the day of Moses.

When God sees the blood of Jesus Christ,

All first fruits are called out of the grave and raised from the dead.

The gift of salvation is summoned,

For the Passover remains the holy convocation.

Do this in remembrance of Jesus Christ.

Take and eat and drink from the cup of salvation.

Obedience unto the faith for God's Passover prayer. Amen.

Life's Interlude

Be I laid not for death

Death is never complete in this world.

That life lives on coming from generation and generation,

Past to present,

With a key to future life from ancestries of our forbearers.

But now, I'm at eternal rest and my life contributes mankind.

Peace of darkness in the shadow of death.

Rest in death,

For that life is a lighted star who welcomes in present life.

For God is God, the Almighty God.

His will be done.

That I foresee not the form of life and see not from death,

For I see life and death as you.

A living person, being blessed with life, what a blessed gift.

Life.

Amen.

God is the Glory

Praise God Saints! His Glory is presence.

To God be the glory, for God is the glory.

Glory unto God. Glory to glory,

From glorification to sanctification,

In glorified praise, let the glory of the church be in the glory of our Lord,

Jesus Christ.

Saints, we are here to praise and worship God in spirit and truth;

For God loves His saints to worship Him truly and freely in the spirit of

Liberty.

God protects all His children.

Therefore, it is not good to persecute the saints of God

Nor grieve the Holy Spirit of God.

Blessed it is to be for God and not against.

Sin is evil and it is the enemy of God;

For where there is holiness, the Spirit of the Holy Ghost ministers unto our

Souls in fellowship with the spirit of hospitality.

Through faith, we worship in Christ's sacred bonds by the

Spirit of the Holy Ghost;

For we know the church is the manifold wisdom of God.

We are governed by grace to be in one accord in the faith of Christ.

Saints, we are full of love.

So, there is love here at our church as we fellowship.

We know love and God is love and we are loved.

But, if anyone cries to one's hurt by anyone of the congregation to not be loved in hostility, let it be known to the elder.

There must be accountability for the body of Christ.

There is spiritual significance in all children of God,

For there is no respecter of person.

We are not to place anyone over God.

No person, nor position to the right or left is

Greater than Jesus who is the head.

We shall reach the broken and lost when they come to our doors.

Let us know how to discern to receive God's people.

Because, saints, we now live in this day where there has come to be a

Hard thing to find a true church in God's Spirit and in the power of the

Holy Ghost in the love of Jesus Christ.

This is real, saints. Therefore, we must not play church because church

Is God's gift.

For the church is the glory of God to be perfected by the souls of the

Children of God.

Every saint has a voice to praise God in godly order.

But Diotrephes, who desires the pre-eminence and power, refuses to

receive the Apostle

John as he wrote to the church (3 John 9).
A mother of two disciples of Christ asked if her sons could be first on the right and left hand position in the kingdom of God.
Let us welcome our visitors in the name of Christ.
We must not be charged that we pushed our visitors out.
We may be entertaining God's angels as the Spirit comes.
We must esteem one another and yet be watchful and prayerful
Against false teachers and antichrist;
The culprit in the pulpit.
Jeremiah 23.1 KJV says, "WOE be unto the pastors that destroy and scatter the sheep of my pasture! saith the Lord".
Mark 9.3 –37 KJV says, "... If any man desire to be first, *the same* shall be last of all, and servant of all. And he took a child, and set him in the midst of them: and when he had taken him in his arms, he said unto them, whosoever shall receive one of such children in my name, receiveth me:
And whosoever shall receive me, receiveth not me, but him that sent me".
Leadership in all saints and pastors, discipleship of Christ is membership of the body.
Companionship is the love of Christ.
Fellowship is inspired for the unity of Christ.

To esteem the least is to be of great leadership in relationship to Christ
Having obedience unto the faith.
Grace's covenant
In the law of faith,
The kingdom of God is here.
Judgment rings majesty.
Repentance comes by faith in the newness of life.
The church is God's gift of praise
For the spirit of the Word.
God is the Word of Life and the Word is the Spirit of God.
A prayer of praise praying in the Holy Ghost;
For His glory, honor and truth. Let us be worthy vessels of honor. For salvation is our gift from God.
Therefore, we give testimonies of praises and glory unto the Lord, our God. Amen.

The Spirit of Father's Day

The spirit of Father's Day to God be the glory.

Holy Spirit of life.

Our Father which art in heaven

Hallowed be Thy name.

Thy name is sanctified and glorified above the earth and the heavens.

Thy kingdom come unto Thy will. Holy Father, holy seed of life is blessed.

This solemn day is sanctified for the glory of our Holy Father.

Good father, you are blessed and holy.

Blessed be the day of the Lord.

For God who is our Father of heaven.

Who is our spirit and truth?

Where is your testimony of faith? Where is the fear of the Lord?

Said the Lord, our God. Holy Father.

I am, I am, I am Lord and Savior, Jesus Christ.

Know ye not your Father who art in heaven and earth

Who provides your daily needs?

Who is thy first fruit?

Whose day is full of light and glory?

For the day of salvation is through God's grace and mercy.

Day by day is given unto us. It is He who gives. Our Holy Father is our gift.

Our new day and new birth is come unto the day of judgement and justice.

Forgiveness and rest are given unto justification and fortification,
For the visitation is to the recompensed.
This day unfolds eternity, for eternal life is the grace of salvation.
From purification is unto perfection in the spirit.
Given by the Spirit of the Father on the day of the Lord.
To God be the glory.
In the name of the Father, the Son, Jesus Christ, and the Holy Ghost
To whom is our Holy Spirit of life.
For the spirit of Father's Day is the kingdom of God.
To God be the glory
Amen.

The Father I Pray To Be

I never cease praying to God, asking Him to direct me in how to become the father I pray to be. I believe and pray that my prayers are in agreement and in obedience to God's will. Certainly, I learned it is not easy to be the best father you desire to be. I find it necessary to pray to God for guidance, direction and instruction to help me be a father to lead my children and family.

I believe prayer will inspire the love of my children's heart to receive me from prison in the near future. I certainly regret not being personally active and involved with my children this present day. Evidently, the physical separation between a father and his family, as in my case, is a loss to everyone.

However, this is a critical life tragedy, which has threatened a permanent separation between my children and me. My absence has unbalanced their lives and personal development. I am therefore in prayer to God to forgive me of my transgressions, sins and crimes against God and my family. I am thankful to God that He has blessed me with the proper father's love to improve our family relationships in the near future. In my prayers, I give thanks to God that my children know I am in prison and that they have forgiven me of my sins. Surely, my fatherly prayers have been significant in my family unity.

Truly, I love my children and I believe every child must experience his father's love. A child who experiences the nature of his father's love ultimately has balance in his life. I find it hard being incarcerated, because I am not providing that responsibility to my children such as the day-to-day interaction a child and a father have to affirm and confirm their personal identities. Unfortunately, each day welcomes them to the unknown. I left my children with unanswered questions. Soon, I pray to reunite with my children. For this cause, I continue to pray that God support them by His Holy Spirit in all areas of their lives while I am absent.

Subsequently, the only direction I can offer my children is in prayer. It is essential that their lives be directed, guided and protected by God. Finally, the responsibilities of a father never cease but in my case inappropriate behavior has limited my capacity to offer my fatherly bonds of nurture and development which is necessary for every healthy child.

Consequently, I have given my love, support and direction to my children. I thank God for giving me the understanding that these spiritual and emotional values are needed for my children to continue their development. Today, it is clear to me that I have transformed from rriy own irresponsibility into a responsible father with loving concern, support and direction for my family. Therefore, I pray to God to remember His Word in my heart to direct me to be a better father; which I pray to be. Amen.

The Anointed of the Holy Spirit

The Holy Spirit of God's anointing grace who is our Lord and Savior, Jesus Christ;
Who is anointed and inspired in the worthiness of faith to do the Ministry of the Holy Ghost.
For the anointed is anointed by grace through the Holy Spirit In the spirit of truth.
The Holy Ghost sanctifies and quickens the spirit of the anointed,
For the head of Jesus Christ is covered and His body is covered by the Holy Spirit's anointing.
The anointed are covered spirit to spirit and faith to faith
Of the Father, our God, who is our sovereignty,
Of the Son, our Lord, Jesus Christ, who is our supremacy of the Holy Ghost who is our authority,
And of the church, the body of Christ, who are the anointed saints of God. Hallelujah.
The anointed saints are prepared with a heart of circumcision To receive the anointing of grace.
The anointed are inspired in the worthiness of faith to walk in the Spirit of grace and mercy.
The kingdom of God is sought first by the anointed in the gift of holiness,
For the Holy Spirit's anointing dwells in the holy temple of grace.

The anointed are the saints of God who are the kingdom heirs
Governed in heavenly places in Jesus
Christ our Savior and Bishop of our soul,
For the anointed live for the things of truth according to the
Fruit of the Spirit.
The anointed are in the spirit of love, grace, faith and the peace of
Jesus Christ with all goodness and meekness of joy;
For God's love anoints these blessings to fill the
Spirit by the power of love.
These blessings are the keys of heaven. They are the gospel of salvation.
For the anointing secures all keys of heaven to bind the spirit of the
Word in the spirit of liberty.

The Spirit of God summons souls to be saved.

You are saved today saints,

For the gift of salvation remains in the kingdom of God.
For the kingdom of glory shines above fully and purely in the authority of
The anointing.
The anointing pours unto the anointed.
Thy kingdom heirs are perfected and covered by *God's* anointing grace.
The anointed are sealed by grace in the Holy Spirit.
The anointed glorifies God in worship and praise by the anointed living
Word of the Holy Spirit.

Salvation is God's anointing grace,
For the anointed is sanctified through the gift of sanctification.
God's anointing grace spiritually shields and seals the safeguards of the Promised union in Jesus Christ,
For the anointed are present in the Holy Spirit by grace.
The Holy Spirit counsels in comfort and warmth with Sincerity of good faith.
Truly, there is hope and joy in God's presence for the anointed.
The anointing powers of virtue are poured unto vessels of Christ;
They are full of praises and prayers unto the voices of praise and joy.
Be anointed and touched by Jesus's helm with faith Whose portions running over in mighty
Fortitude in the sword of the Word having the oneness in Jesus Christ.
For the anointing seals grace and mercy to unction the Spirit by the urgency of love.
God's anointing empowers spiritual unction in majestic praises forever in The glory of holiness. Amen.

God's Temple Endures Satan's Temptation

We are not of ourselves but, we are temples of grace;
For God's anointed Word speaks true testimonies of salvation.
The living temples of prayer and praise witnessed these truths,
Who comes near when souls are saved and called.
There is justice, justification and judgment in righteousness.
Saints are tried by the fire of the Holy Ghost.
But Satan is the tempter, who is the falling flame of temptation,
Who is in the spirit of disobedience,
Deception, rebellion, control, contradiction, and seduction
To steal, to kill, and to destroy souls.
Who tests the worthiness of your faith and your spirituality.
Saints are justified by faith and by the Word of God.
There is no spiritual unity of God and Satan nor good and evil.
Jesus' saints are the temple of God,
For the true worshipper is verified by the covenant of truth.
God's temple is where the kingdom of God dwells.
This is where the living Spirit of the Holy Ghost remains in our hearts.
Temples of love by the grace of our Lord Jesus Christ,
Who overcomes evil temptation and the children of disobedience,
Who walks in the Spirit and not in the lust of the flesh.

He stands in the holy place to hear our prayers, and praise
In times of crisis, fear, evil, and sin, when our spirituality is tested
By temptation.
Spirituality overcomes sensuality.
Blessed be the soul who endures temptation
By the sword of the Word of God for your good will not be
Evil spoken of.
Holiness secures the Word to follow after Christ.
In my weakness, God's Word is my strength to overcome trials and
Temptations.
God's eternal word is endurance and Holy Ghost power.
This endurance lasts to the end of temptation.
To worship Satan is to worship a false god without power and
Authority.
The love of sin is the root of evil in disobedience.
Endurance is without breaking the saints' integrity who remain
To bear the pains of distress is to bear the suffering of Christ.
The believer yields not unto sin but remains whole in heart to Christ.
Christ is your loyalty and allegiance in the keeper of the faith,
For the glory of the Lord Jesus Christ endures forever.
God's temple endures over Satan's temptation. Amen.

A Kiss in the Rain

By faith, the rain of joy pours downward from heaven softly
As spring days fill one's heart
And summer gives birth anew in the spirit of grace
By faith.
For this godly kiss in the rain seals promise love
When peace never ceases.
Jesus kisses me with His anointing grace,
He breathes the sanctity of a true kiss by faith
Thank you, Jesus Christ, for your holy kiss
Praises are ever joy
Holiness and virtue couple in the joys of peace.
When a kiss is in the rain by faith, given freely from the heart,
This kiss in the rain sanctifies the testimonies of love.
By faith, mercy and grace rest unto the treasures of stars in heaven
And angels lift the praises of faith in God,
For the heirs of salvation.
By faith, heavenly love is for you in the kingdom of God.
Immediately, my love,
As we kiss in the rain tonight, in the glory of God's light
It is so right and bright without a fight or our might.
As the wind blows softly in the heat of spring, in heaven's mist by faith,

Our spirit bears witness in the reverie of our hearts' delight.

Rebirth, rejoice, restore.

By faith,

Who prepares us for joining together?

One man and one woman.

By faith,

One sealed kiss in the rain walking, breathing, and smiling in the rain.

As we kiss this sweet kiss, in the spirit of faith,

Inspired living and thinking good things,

Giving thanks to God for His gift of love in Jesus

Our kiss of grace

By faith. Amen.

I Know Secrets

Secrets of depths

Thoughts of vision

A portrait of silence

What notion, like the oceans that embrace that earth and kiss this sky

Where rainbow bridges reaches you and me

That notion, a portrait of silence,

Thoughts of vision what distinguish me

In Spirit, my soul and heart,

My humanity

In portrait vision, secrets of depths

Thoughts of things that be.

I know secrets, Almighty God,

Things that You know, which is no secret to me. Amen.

The Pastor's Wife

The pastor's wife is an inspired woman of grace.
She is a virtuous woman who is inspired in the worthiness of faith.
She is her husband's crown and jewel in one accord.
They are heart to heart and faith to faith.

The pastor's wife is thy beloved lady of holiness
Who is thy first lady who adorns herself in the beauty of holiness.
Who stands on God's promised word.
She is a God-fearing woman who is led by the Holy Spirit.
Sweet lady beloved in kindness and love in the ministries of faith.

The pastor's wife is blessed with the spirit of hospitality.
Sweet gentle spirit of loveliness praying in the Holy Ghost.
She is blessed with her heart of godliness in the spirit of understanding,
For the pastor's wife is God's promised gift to her husband.

She is the pastor's delight and joy after God's own heart.
She is a virtuous woman pleasing God and her husband with her first
Fruits,
For the light of glory is revealed and the power of the gospel is
Relieved.

She believes in the true gospel of faith through our Lord, Jesus Christ.
She is her husband's crown of love that his eyes shine with sparkling Delight.
A wife of God's covenant,
She is a lady of faithfulness.
In understanding spiritual things.
She is a God-fearing woman anointed and ordained by the Holy Spirit.

In the Spirit of God, she prays and worships God truly in thy Faithfulness,
For the Holy Spirit is the substance of her strength and faith.

In the spirit of hospitality,
Beloved lady blessed you from exhortation to edification.
In the fear of the Lord, our God,
She kneels her head unto God's throne of grace,
For she esteems others greater than herself;
Who encourages and edifies their soul with humbleness.

The gift of salvation calls unto her in answered prayers.
Her faith is full of virtue in the Spirit of God's wisdom and love.
In honor of our beloved pastor's wife,
May the blessings of God bless you in the name of Jesus Christ. Amen.

God's Holy Gift

Immediately, God brings forth His gift in Jesus
As a full seed in Godspeed
In His creation lives the ready seed
Rightly planted in every need
Is called
To yield praises abundantly
From sanctification to glorification
Reverence unto God, the giver of gifts
The gift of the Holy Ghost in love, grace, mercy and faith
The gifted seed indeed
Obedience responds joyfully
In thanksgiving for His Holy gift
Directly believing in Jesus' creed
His propitiation for our sin
Mercy appeases atone
As Jesus healing blood bleeds
His blood we drink and His bread we eat
We feed
We nourish deeply and search and seek
We come promptly in obedience

Quickly rooted in Jesus' love and faith

We receive His gift gracefully

His gift of life whose values are greater than earthy treasure.

We rejoice

God breathe in thy Holy birth

God's children's life begins the gift of the spirit.

For the gift of God is eternal life.

Immediately, in riches, wealth with the Holy Ghost power,

No other treasure is above grace's tower.

How meek thy seed keeps

In the gift of charity, kindness, temperance, patience, generosity and truthfulness

As a humble soul who weeps

To live in holiness as salvation's words steeps

Tears of faith from a gifted heart

Discerning righteously in Jesus Christ,

For the spiritual gift truly encourages others and builds them up.

God's gift in thy mouth for speech

To preach and to teach

Confess now and testify

In thy Word of Truth and spirit

With obedience through the Spirit of God

These times are urgent, saints.

Neglect not thy gift. Resist the Devil,

For the hour of Christ is so near.

In the day and in the night

Just before she sleeps and her wink

Of an eye gives no peep

Jesus' salvation calls and judgement keeps

Her destiny

There will your soul answer Jesus

Sweet promises of eternal rest

Souls are repented, rescued, redeemed and consoled best

The gift of forgiveness before the test

Trusts in His faith

Being healed in Jesus Christ's quiet strength and peace

His gift of salvation and holiness

Amen

The Good Fight of Faith

A minister of Christ must be prepared to fight the good fight of faith by keeping a heart of godliness and faith consciences to take hold and to defend the Word of God. He defends God's Word by sound gospel doctrine, having trustworthiness, honor and most of all the soul of prayer. The minister is to be above any reproach, respectable and hospitable to others. He is nourished in the word of faith to reveal the gospel light of eternal life of salvation to which this is called and by every steward making good confession in the presence of many witnesses before God (1Tim. 6:1-23).

The minister ought to be of good courage in his measure of faith. His measure of faith is established only to please God. Jesus blesses and says, "Put on the full armor of God so that you will be able to stand firm against the schemes of the devil" (Eph.6:11 NASB). The minister's faith in Jesus resists all temptations and schemes of the devil. The minister reveals spiritual significance in his personal testimony which testifies and demonstrates the glory of good conscience and perseverance in doing the service of God's will.

There is a sense of urgency that the minister requires full faith in the Holy Spirit to declare his walk with the Lord. His Faith in Jesus justifies and gives promise through the living Spirit of God. Therefore, the minister is reassured in continuance faith throughout all trials in the mission of Christ as his faithful witness and servant answering to God's call of mercy and grace. Amen.

God's Holy Light of Glory

God's Holy Spirit reveals God's holy light of glory.
The authority of the Holy Ghost governs the holy light of glory in Truth and spirit.
Through the revelation of the light of truth,
His Spirit bears witness in holiness, and righteousness;
For God is our holy living light of glory from Justification to glorification.
Through faith, the law of the light is ordained and anointed by the Word of God.
By the power of blessings, the light illuminates the Word of God.
Jesus Christ is the light of our salvation and He is our soul's delight,
For God is the glorious light who reigns in the authority of the Holy Spirit.
Through mercy and grace, the children of light have the Armor of light in the gospel.
In the gospel, God's light of glory transforms the dead in sin into life Unto righteousness;
For there is sanctity in God's light of glory.
In the excellency of grace, the glory of the Lord. Our God fills our Hearts with the power of truth.

In the fear of the Lord, Jesus is the light who draws my soul and spirit to testify in spirit and truth;

For the truth is the way of the light in our Lord, Jesus Christ, and the spirit is the life of salvation;

The consoler of the light of consolation who inspires the Spirit.

Let God's light shine in your hearts and know

Who enlightens the eyes of your hearts.

Jesus Christ is the way to the indwelling light for

I yield all my might unto God's will, way and word in worship.

In the ministry of faith, He is the promised light who is the light of Deliverance.

Let us walk in the holy light of glory.

Let our souls be the light of glory in the

Flaming ministries of the spirit,

For God's holy light of glory is present in the fire of Holy Ghost. The light is Holy Ghost power unto you in the glory of God. Amen.

Prayer

In the sanctification of faith, we are praying in Jesus' peace.
Praying in the fire baptism of the Holy Ghost.
Being filled in the Holy Spirit and praying in the Holy Ghost.
Praying in the healing power of the Holy Ghost.
Believing in the miracles of God.
Sharing in the love of God, we are caring for every soul.
Giving God all the glory and honor for His forgiving grace.
Thanking God for the Spirit of the Holy Ghost's intercession.
We are hoping and trusting in God's word in answering our prayers.
Obeying and loving God for our love walk by faith.
Walking hand by hand for the deliverance of the gospel.
Seeing eye to eye the things faith is doing in our lives
And hearing the melodies of grace psalms in our hearts of praise.
Calling on the name of God in one accord, Yahweh, our Lord.
Soul to soul, faith to faith, spirit to spirit, heart to heart.
Knowing the Word of God in our hearts.
Testifying unto the crown of glory in Jesus Christ our Lord and Savior.
Amen

Jesus is the Way of the Spirit

Behold, I am the way of the spirit of God, for my Father and I are one.
Our ways are one in the Holy Spirit.
We witness our testimonies in the spirit of truth.
The word of life is the way of the Father, the Son and the Holy Spirit.
O my soul, bless the Lord and hear what the Spirit says in the way of the Word of God.
Listen to the Spirit of God and hear the glory of truth calls your name.
God's voice is an irresistible call to obedience, repentance and Reconciliation.
Behold, my child, consider your ways.
I preach and teach you my ways of love in mighty words and Deeds to lead the way.
I prepare your heart to reach you in prayer and worship and answer your name to my will.
Consider your ways for they are not of the Father.
Your ways are in the sin of disobedience, transgression, and rebellion.
Your ways are obeying the lust of the flesh, the lust of the eye and the Pride of life.
To hear is to obey God's voice in word and deed, for obedience bears Witness.

By My name, you may be redeemed and restored unto Me;
For my ways are justice and righteousness in the spirit of truth.
For I am the way in the light of truth.
I am holy and sanctified by my word of life.
My ways are my words; for they are pure, sure and true.
Consider your ways for thy soul is required.
Thy soul has an obligation to love and obey God in worship, praise and Honor.
We are thankful to sanctify thy soul and bless God,
For Jesus is the way of the Spirit of God. Amen.

A Faithful Hearer of God's Word Listens Obediently

In prayer, a faithful hearer of God's word communes and worships God
By ordained authority.
To obey through the benevolence of God's Word is to express the good
Faith of God.
In praises and honor unto God, the faithful hearer listens obediently and
Submits to obedience.
There the hearer's benediction ushers the spirit of grace and mercy in
Conforming to God's will.
When the faithful hearer listens obediently and lovingly, obedience
Expresses obligation unto God.
Love is a required obligation unto the obedience of God's Word.
Obedience bears witness to hearing faith.
Obedience yields to the binding power of God's voice in righteousness.
I do hear and obey God in reverence.
In the fear of the lord, God opens and prepares the heart of the ear to
Hear His sweet still voice.
In the Spirit of the Holy Ghost, the heart and soul in man declare God's
Word to live by faith.
God's voice calls the heart in man to truthfully and honestly hear God's
Voice.

The faithful hearer of God's word is ready and prepared to listen and
Receive God's spoken word.
She learns, by faith, in believing God to follow God's will, word, ways and
Work with full trust.
A faithful hearer is a faithful doer unto the will of God.
In glory, obedience gives consent and trust to God's Word.
In comeliness, the hearer consents to the blessings of spiritual healings
And blessings of the will of God.
A faithful hearer of God's word listens obediently and diligently;
For the spirit to receive spiritual things, the spirit of wisdom,
understanding and knowledge is applied.
A faithful hearer is a faithful doer.
Those who give their ear to God shall perceive and consider things in faith
With God's understanding,
As a living witness, one who perfects obedience unto God's
Commandments.
Jesus Christ's voice speaks unto you and His voice comes unto you to be
Relieved. Amen.

God's Gift of Hope

To whom is your hope? Where is your hope?

In hopelessness, repented souls come to God in the spirit of hope.

To whom God has given you spiritual hope is to your live in the Word of God.
In hope, there is worship and praise given unto God's holy name.
There are seasons of hope from grace to mercy.
Let the cheer of hope be your victory unto safety in the will of God.
God's gift of hope is given freely in the spirit of liberty.
To whom much is given onto our vessel is to much is required of our souls
Where is your tenacity of hope? Why do you hold on to hope?
The reliability of hope receives the accountability of hope.
To this end, Jesus Christ is God's gift of hope unto salvation.
He is God's gift of hope from the promised Word of God.
Without hope, there is no freedom, no faith and no freedom.
There is spiritual significance in the virtue of hope.
When hope comes, there is the anointed power of the Holy Spirit.
Jesus Christ is the pre-eminence and head of hope.
My soul strives in God's gift of hope
My soul receives God's gift of hope in obedience of faith.
My soul believes and trusts in thy hope.

My soul relieves freedom of joy in Jesus' hope.
My spirit yields unto God.
In prayer, God ushers in the spirit of hope.
For the Holy Ghost works in our hearts through the Word of God.
Therefore, hope is the assurance of God's mercy and grace.
For hope proclaims liberty and victory over the spirit of Satan's power of sin and death.
Who is our hope?
Jesus Christ is my gift of promised hope. Jesus' hope is solid, secured, safe, and stable
Upon every Word of God who speaks in the spirit of hope
God welcomes His Holy Spirit in the spirit of hope.
The presence of God gives hope unto our spirit; acknowledged hope in the wisdom of God.
Give hope.
Give God's hope to your loved ones, to your enemies and to your neighbors
The value of hope tests in times of patience
Give hope for faith healings in prayer.
Hope purifies and cleanses the soul in the leap of faith.
There is great expectation in the excellence of the spirit of hope,
For hope yields the harvest of faith;
For hope removes the sorrows of sin and guilt.

The charity of hope gives honesty and integrity.

Hope opens hospitality and humility for capability in God's forgiveness.

The power of hope is Jesus Christ unto all authority

Hope deceives not, nor grieves or deprives.

To believe in hope and to receive the gift of God is to be relieved in the Glory of God.

Let us glorify God in God's spirit of worship and praise with the hope of The Holy Spirit in Jesus Christ. Amen.

Christmas Prayer

O Holy Father God, we sing our prayers in remembrance of Jesus Christ in
The Spirit of the Holy Ghost.
The announcement of the Christ is come.
Grace and peace have blessed this day our Savior has come.
That Jesus Christ whom we have given our praises and thanksgivings for
His mercy and grace.
In word and deed, thy kingdom comes yielding the fruits of the Spirit and
Magnifying the God of glory.
We say hosanna and bring festivity in gifts to honor the light of Jesus,
The King
Who is the living light, the anointed Christ.
Forgive us, Father, for our words are near but our hearts are
Uncircumcised.
Let our voices ring together calling on God's name, Immanuel,
For we know God is with us.
Jesus comes by the holy gift of the Holy Ghost in the fire and water of
His blood to save souls;
Who freely gives us the gift of salvation.
Jesus is the miracle virgin birth who is our sign of
God who is the crown of glory,

For heaven witnesses this day in obedience unto God.
We pray in having the hope and patience to such a time in our Sabbath rest.
Jesus ministers healings by the seed of the gospel and worships God in Spirit and truth.
The saints of God fellowship in love relationship by the membership to Christ.
Thank God that Jesus is our anointed Christ who is the light of Love, joy and hope
Who is our mediator and intercessor for our transgression of sin?
For Jesus Christ is the righteousness of God through the justification in Faith,
By His birth, life, death, burial, resurrection and ascending unto the Kingdom of God.
There our Christmas prayer is to have the virtue and substance of Jesus Christ in our walk of life.
Prayer for a new day on a new earth.
From the great valleys of forgiveness to the mountain tops of Redemption and above,
The galaxies of sanctification where the love of holy faith welcomes God's holy kingdom.
In the heavens, there is a time where all seasons meet;

The winter, spring, summer and fall, to say
Holy blessings and season greetings
With Christmas cheer and faith
Let Christmas be more than a time and place
But more unity of Christ in our hearts where the
Priceless treasure remains in
God's glory by His honor, joy, mercy and grace after God's own heart.
We pray this holy Christmas prayer in Jesus Christ, our Savior's name, for
His remembrance.
To our holy Father, Yehovah Yahweh, in the Holy Spirit. Amen

Fasting Faith

There is holy anointed faith in God our Holy Father.

In the kingdom of God, my soul and spirit are sanctified in fasting faith.

Blessed grace for praying in the will of God.

Thank you, heavenly Father, for our union of praying grace.

In the beauty of holiness and faith, I believe in the holy things of God.

My anointed faith calls God in my obedience.

In thy holy name, Jesus Christ is present in thy glory.

I humbly kneel by grace to come forth unto Jesus Christ's feet in faith.

In heavenly things of God, thy gift of faith is the seed of grace.

In grace and mercy, fasting faith is abstaining from all sin and all evil of the Devil by Jesus' word and deed;

Who freed and delivered your soul from sin and cleansed you from the Death spirit of unbelief.

God's salvation covenant is unto life and eternal grace.

In the blood of Jesus Christ, who comes by the holy gift of the holy fire And water of the Holy Ghost;

Perfecting grace and sanctifying in the Holy Spirit

In thankfulness and gratefulness our souls in Christ Jesus are forever.

There is new life in the kingdom of God by the victory of Christ Jesus.

Fasting faith in Jesus Christ is empowered by the Gospel.

There is fasting faith through his birth, life, death, resurrection and Ascending unto the kingdom of God.

Jesus Christ is in the Holy Ghost power to do the will of God.

In the spirit of truth, Jesus promises life and salvation for the children of God who follow the will of God.

Fasting faith is the obedience to God in trust and belief in our lord Jesus Christ to follow him.

Here we are in prayer and fasting faith for the love of God. Amen.

A Mother's Prayer on Mother's Day

Dear Lord God, my love in prayer who my soul loves. My life begins from Your Spirit. May my love please You beyond the shallow of the grave. Truly, I pray thee to be a mother of victory and virtue in the blessings of your faith, and trust. Here, I do repent my sins in fasting faith.

Yes, Lord, I am with child in my womb. Please remember my child all the days of his life; saving his soul beyond the captivity of sin's pit of prison, of death, of the lost. Permit me, Lord, to have the strength to be connected in the manner worthy to be a good mother as I weaned and reared up my child (Prov. 23:13, 29:17). I solemnly give thanks to you, Lord Jesus, for the fruit of thy seed to do Your will and to please You in truth, spirit and faith in You (Luke 1:42).

For an example, Hannah exemplifies these virtues. She echoes these virtues in 1 Samuel 1:26-27. Here "And she said Oh my Lord, as thy soul liveth, my lord, I *am* the woman that stood by thee here, praying unto the Lord. For this child I prayed; and the Lord hath given me my petition which I asked of him". Redeem me, I pray to come home to you with promise.

Please allow me Lord to know how to have true value in the freedom of motherhood in my children's lives. May I be spiritually touched in maturity before the moment of conception to the beginning of each month I bare in my pregnancy (Jer. 1:5, Ps.71:6). Bless me Lord when I give birth to see my child grow.

For my child is beautiful and proper, "For thou hast possessed my reins: thou hast covered me in my mother's womb" (Ps. 139:13). Cleanse me in your love dear Lord, for I truly believe in Your gospel and I love You.

Let me have the strength to catch my child before he falls to correct him and to save him from evil, in only your strength Lord, I do pray. Let me give my presence to be near his soul to pick him up if he falls, to encourage his first footsteps and to support him along the way. Let me be there to push his little feet when he begins to crawl, and to hold his little hands when he begins to stand and to walk.

Enable me to have the ears to listen to him from his heart when he begins to speak his first words. Enable me to know when he is in trouble and needs encouragement. Touch my heart Lord to know when he is sick and when he needs healing, hunger and feeding, thirst and drinking and all his other needs to be fulfilled.

Let me teach him accurately according to Your Word and have a bonding trustworthy relationship sealed with soundness, security, safeness and stability in a home of comfort; that I may provide these needs for my children in all things in your grace only; that I shall never fail to be a good mother to the highest respect through all seasons: from the spring of youth to the winter of aged maturity.

Let me be alert and sound in mind, soul and spirit in all times as well as he. May I be truly honored as a godly mother of your love and virtue. Let me be truly worthy of your Spirit in Christ. Let me humble myself in childbirth faithfully in your grace. Please have mercy on me in your sight. Please give me faithful courage to face my spiritual destiny of salvation and to be able to gracefully discern in balance my integrity in temperance, knowledge, wisdom and prudence within every degree of equity. Now Lord prepare my heart to have these portions of measure to enable me to fear you in reverence, truth, honor and spiritual worship.

Focus my mind to be a visionary in the promise of hope in your image Jesus Christ. Grant me your promise in the Gospel. Direct my soul to understand these virtues of the fruit of the Spirit. Perceive in me your spiritual kingdom of reality in my soul with humility and ability. May I be keen in discerning the spirit of my child.

Strengthen me, Lord, to carry this new life as growth brings him unto deliverance. In my eyes, I see this young soul being one of the greatest gifts from my womb to birth. May I have greater hope in you, Lord, that my child shall please You in Jesus' faith (Exod. 2:2; Heb. 11:23).

Truly my child is more excellent than myself. May my peace be full of joy of Christ. Now my smiles are beyond the pains and struggles through childbirth and delivery because I know You are ever present Lord in my every need. For You Lord promise that mother "notwithstanding she shall be saved in childbearing, if they continue in faith and charity and holiness with sobriety" (1 Tim. 2:15). Now, I rest with a mother's melody in speech and motherhood of maternal love having a watchful eye and my hand giving care in prayer as I kneel to Thee in faith who touches me in grace.

I have seen glory on the face of my great grandmother whom I honored. Grant me Lord God the patience to shine the radiance of a mother's beauty of content as my children grow in good health from a tender young heart. I now understand a virtuous mother's worthiness is beyond compare for no other mother ever come near in the eyes of her own child.

A grown child can appreciate this mother's diligence and compassion which is always given. I remembered my mother's merciful might in loving words and deeds according to the spirit of grace in love, joy, peace, long suffering, gentleness, goodness, faith, sincerity, trust, obedience, meekness, godliness, with a balance of temperance, knowledge, wisdom, prudence, holiness, honor and equity in truth.

I fully witnessed my mother clothed in these fruits of spiritual virtues having the fear of the Lord our God. Indeed, my mother gracefully stands and walks as I see her as tall as the heavenly skies in my heart. No others shall measure to the degree to what my mother means to me particularly in substance and quality (Gal.5:22-23; Pr.1.1; Ps.139:14).

I know mother that you are purely rare in the beauty of God's anointing always giving praises unto God for life. Yet, you have given all that you have bared up unto God's care and without regards to a respecter of persons. Once again, Hannah echoes her concerns in prayer that her petition be granted from the Lord. In 1 Samuel 1:27 she says, "For this child I prayed; and the Lord hath given me my petition which I asked of him" in accordance to your will. Now, my mother's heart is delighted as in Elkannah's wife, Hannah. Moreover, in 1 Samuel 2:1 KJV Hannah's declaration proclaims the glory in God "And Hannah prayed, and said my heart rejoiceth in the Lord; mine horn is exalted in the Lord;

My mouth is enlarged over mine enemies because I rejoice in thy salvation". For salvation unto her is the kingdom of God purely in her heart that her child gives glory unto the Lord our Lord and Savior of our soul.

Therefore, our mothers, brothers, and sisters and saints have counseled us with the love of Christ in His image is such a true vision of life. So she envisions and understands these virtues in the honor of life. Thus, perceiving life in humility with discerning spirit to each child. May salvation in God be our mother's gift today. I love you, mother. Happy Mother's Day in prayer for your dedication and love. Amen.

The Virtuous Woman

Who is inspired by God's Holy Spirit
She is God's gift and crown to man.
Fully in God's will and Spirit, she honors her virtue in Jesus' faith.
She stands on God's promised words and works.
Who is secured in the integrity of holiness.
In her virtue, holiness witnesses her thoughts in words,
Ways, works and will.
A living testimony acceptable unto God by grace and mercy
Being a pleasing soul unto God.
The virtuous woman,
Her faith is full of virtue in the Spirit of God,
For God knows the heart of a virtuous woman.
Her heart is great in diligence and depth.
Who is holy and gracious by God's faithful Spirit.
The virtuous woman spiritually understands her issues of life.
She knows they are issues from the heart of God.
Her gift to life is in the glory of joy.
She is a cheerful witness by faith.
In God, her faithful strength is established.
Her beauty is the song of praise giving God the glory.
She is completely a beautiful woman.

She knows her purposes and substances are God's gifts.
A humble spirited heart is cleansed,
Saved and delivered from sin.
Her heart is sound, stable, secure and safe in God's love.
Her speech is a truthful tongue whose pleasant words
Flow from her mouth.
Hearing faith for justice and truth, her speech is with
Sweetness of lips.
Who is a sweet jewel to my soul
Having lips of understanding and knowledge in the fear of God.
Her wisdom speaks in her soul of prayer.
In prayers, she gives all praises of gratefulness in
Thanksgivings and forgiveness.
Love and grace ministered her hands through the power of the
Holy Spirit.
Her touch works miracles of faith which are blessed in
Goodness and mercy.
She is my delight and rejoice.
A wife of my covenant and a heart of understanding,
Wisdom and knowledge of God.
The light of her eyes shine so clearly from her heart with
Compassion in the ministries of faith.

She is a gracious woman who retains honor.

Who is the crown of my glory in God.

A virtuous woman and helpmeet.

A deliverer of grace by the Holy Spirit.

Who knows the heart of God.

A virtuous woman.

Time

God's gift of time is the time of times
Who is the Alpha and Omega. In God, there is time,
Who is the beginnings and endings of time. Prayer time, saints.
Prayer unfolds eternal time.
Which redeems our time by forgiveness. God is our time.
He is our redeemer of our time.
Prayer reveals the revelations of time,
For time testifies reformation and transfiguration.
This time is at hand.
The season begins for our times and seasons have come.
Yet, time is no longer time.
The hour has come, for judgment justifies this time.
We shall bless the Lord our God at all times through the fullness of times.
There is a time before time. Time times time.
Time by time, time within time,
These are the generations of times past for our journey's
Passages of time in seasons.
The anointed time for time for end times.
The Holy Spirit knows the time of truth,
For the verification of truth shall stand,
For time opens the door to our salvation,

For God welcomes us unto His kingdom, the kingdom of God.
The Spirit of God governs eternal time through Jesus Christ, our Savior.
The perfection of the gospel is completed through the time of grace and Mercy in Jesus Christ.
Time around time, time beyond time, eternal time, are time above times.
Before the heavens and the earth, timeless time remains.
There is time for a season in the Garden of Eden. But sin occurred and Changed our language by time.
To live is life but time is to death.
Our souls require the Spirit of God to live.
In the morning, born of the Holy Spirit for God is pleased of your faith.
Pure faith is worthy of Christ's first gifts of spiritual fruits.
But, the midnight hour is near. The threshold moment is here now.
The promise time is the gift expresses God's covenant of salvation.

Revelation

The flower of time unfolds the unseen time.
What time is it? Time answers time.
The Word of God is the life of the Spirit.
In the light of time, there is prayer for all times.
There comes a time when you are there to praise God worthy of your spirit.
The spirit of faith ministers unto God.

In the sanctity of times, who magnifies the gift of life?

In Jesus' peace the time of blessings and healings.

Eternal times praise in prayer in worshipping God our Holy Father, God.

Through our Lord Jesus Christ in godliness and

Holiness by the kingdom of glory

Who is exalted in all times and eternal time. Jesus' time. Amen.

The Heart of Circumcision

Blessed be the believer's heart of circumcision
Who walks in the integrity of heart.
The Word of God is sealed by
The Spirit of the Holy Ghost in
Truth and spirit.
God prepares the heart to obey His word.
Having the fear of God
With the spirit of counsel and might
To worship in love by the spirit of God's wisdom,
Knowledge and understanding to
Hear the voice of God in the depths of the heart;
For the circumcised heart bears witness to God's trust,
Faith and belief in the spirit of holiness by the
Holy Ghost who sanctifies the God-fearing heart
Through the gift of praise and prayer?
Jesus Christ perfects the hearts of all saints.
His glory gives us the sanctity of grace in faith
To have this heart of circumcision,
For the Lord's true witnesses give true testimonies
Of the circumcised heart.
The heart of circumcision. Amen.

The Circumcised Heart

The voice of conscience speaks both to the wise and unwise.
But, the circumcised heart bears witness to God's trust, faith and belief.
The circumcised heart is in the spirit of truth.
The circumcised heart is
In God's knowledge, wisdom and understanding.
The circumcised heart is a seal of holiness.
The circumcised heart is
In the spirit of holiness of the Holy Ghost;
Testifying the sanctity of the Godhead's heart.
The circumcised heart is
Through the gift of praise and prayer.
Who has spiritual discernment
With the gift of a wise and understanding heart?
The Circumcised heart.
Amen.

Rainbows of Fruit

To smell the rainbow's fruit

And taste the infinity flavors.

I see the sounds of heaven.

Through all forms of life, hearing water breathing.

And blessed with life to feel the colors and see the wind.

O God,

I, too, feel the colors of the wind embracing me.

My heart is in full bloom.

A man with love-hood.

Outward from axis of being inward the world.

Rainbows of fruit from the spirit

The fruit of the Spirit. God's spirit of love.

Amen.

Who is the Shepherd and Savior of our Soul?

Jesus is our Shepherd and Savior of our soul. He is the only Son of God who has faithfully, obediently and perfectly pleased God. His living testaments and scriptural evidences and witnesses are recorded in biblical testimony, words and deeds.

Jesus declares unto us simple truths of revelation. His revelation gives spiritual significance particularly in the area of spiritual salvation for our soul. For this reason, Jesus says in Psalms 40:7 KJV and Hebrew 10:7 KJV, "Then said I, Lo, I come in the volume of the book *it is* written of me, I delight to do thy will, O my God: yea, thy law is within my Heart". The Word of God is the book of the shepherd. To perceive the word of God is to have a heart of God.

Jesus is our Shepherd who provides the eternal gift of salvation. Through forgiveness of sin, God's mercy and grace, He disarms the evil one and redeemed the children of God. God is well pleased. Jesus is the only one whom God exalts to His right hand. We are forever His sheep. However, God is our Creator who owns His sheep through the redemptive blood of Jesus Christ; who has divine sovereignty, supremacy and authority with power to enforce and to direct His creation.

Jesus warns the shepherds and sheep about the un-anointed shepherd of war. This is the warring shepherd. Jesus identifies him who is Satan. Satan is the spiritual father of death. He hides in imperfection. For he is not whole. He does not produce good fruit. It is in his nature to steal, to kill, and to destroy.

In the spirit of death, the false shepherd is inherently all sin being against all righteousness. His works include: adultery, murder, envy, drunkenness, fornication, uncleanness, lasciviousness, idolatry, witchcraft, hatred, variance, emulations, wrath, strife, seditions and heresies. More unrighteousness follows in the form of theft, covetousness, wickedness, deceit, evil eye, blasphemy, pride, foolishness, backbiters, haters of God, inventors of evil things, disobedience to God without understanding and covenant breakers. Sin begets more sin. Obsession, delusion, oppression, depression, secret arts, haughty eyes, shedding of innocent blood, a heart that devises wicked plans, malice, feet that run rapidly run to evil, appeals to false witness, one who spreads strife among unity, and spreads the spirit of laziness, impulsive behavior, distraction, bored, lure appeal to attract bait, uselessness, aggressive resentful, jealous, anxious, despondency, desolation, desperation, worry, inconsistency to truth, mortification, stagnation, fraud, depravity, corruption, recession, discouragement, breaches of trust, captivated, fixated, troubled, compulsion, mania, insane, violent, crisis, perversion, bribe, degrade, adulterate, defile, demoralize, pollute, disguise, injure, damage, confusion, covetous, skepticism, ill-gotten gains, negligence, hatred stirs up strife, pride, dishonor, greed, cruelty, failure, envious, degeneracy, perplexed, misconception, guilt, resentment, hallucination, illusion, misrepresentation, downheartedness, doubt, negative thoughts, unreliability, inaccuracy, untrustworthy, and questionable, defeat, unsecured, unsafe, unstable, all these attributes are spirits of death who belongs to the Devil who deceives in his spirit of evil possession against God's sheep (Rom. 1:28-32, Rom. 6:20, Gal. 5:20-21).

We are our brother's keepers. We must be strong in the Word of God and in the power of God. We must be accountable to one another as we love one another unto God; that we put on the whole armor of God to enable us to stand against the wiles of the Devil (Eph. 6:10-24). Amen.

God's Glory of Restoration

For God is the glory of restoration through our Lord Jesus Christ; who is the sovereignty, the supremacy and the authority in the Holy Spirit. For Jesus Christ is our complete atonement and propitiation from sin of disobedience unto obedience and righteousness. In the unity of the spirit, Jesus Christ ministers the gift of healing to restore the sick and the lost unto restoration and reconciliation of men release from the wrath of sin unto the Holy Father of God; for Jesus is the life and the light of men. The light through the light who is the glory of God. For men to know God is to call upon Him in reverence and sincerity with the voice of cheer and gladness with thanksgiving grace. For God knows the heart of men and women of restoration. For they are one in the glory of God. For they are God's holy vessels of faith who are cleansed in the Holy Spirit believing on the Son of God.

In the sum of all things, God has replenished the spirit and supplied all things necessary for the deeds of His word in His son Jesus Christ who is our eternal life. For salvation is provided in the abundance of grace through Jesus Christ who is our Savior and Bishop of our souls safe for eternity. In the kingdom of God, Jesus has come to serve and restore the lost from sin through repentance and forgiveness. The men of restoration are to be returned to the kingdom of God because Jesus has the victory.

Jesus has relinquished all strongholds of evil; destroying sin and death. Now, souls are restored unto restoration and reconciliation. They are called to rest whole in the spirit of holiness and the beauty of love. In the beauty of holiness, the spirit is edified for the men of restoration who are quickened, revived, refreshed and made alive.

In the kingdom of God there is restoration unto God's friendship by the peace of righteousness unto Jesus Christ. There is recovery from sin and death unto glory and grace. Through the mercies of God, who has ordained holy men and restored them unto restoration and reconciliation to obey Him and to please Him worthy in love, trust and truth. In the worthiness of faith, they are cleansed from the death spirit of unbelief unto life and unto eternal grace. Where men were dead in their trespasses of sin but, in God's loveliness and godliness, there is spiritual identity and intimacy. In fasting faith and integrity of heart men of restoration are abstaining from all evil and sin. For they believe and trust in Jesus Christ's power of the gospel. For the power of the gospel is of the Holy Ghost.

Therefore, men of restoration who are washed and cleansed thoroughly from their iniquities by the blood of Jesus Christ. In God's presence, these men worship with hearts of circumcision renewed and restored in God's Spirit to fellowship and praise and worship. From sanctification to glorification the spirit is revived. The men of restoration are grateful and fruitful for God's blessings of repentance and forgiveness. Secure in God's salvation in His bosom of grace is the sanctuary for our Sabbath rest. Through the justification of faith and the purification of souls, restored men are called and summoned. For there is redemption unto deliverance and there is restoration unto reconciliation through the justification of grace. Thy help and health are restored. My hope is restored. My spirit is restored. For God is our restorer of healings. He is our healer in all blessings and prayer. The men of restoration are humbled spirits to witness unto God. For God has turned His men back to Him again relieved heirs in the kingdom of God and restored unto the gift of salvation. God's glory of restoration is preeminent. Amen

God's Glory of Strength

In the name of our Holy Father God,

Yah.

Thy name Yah is the sanctuary of glorification and fortification.

Thy strength is clothed and glorified in righteousness of loveliness,

Holiness, and godliness.

O, mighty God, Thy voice speaks power in the joy of Your glory.

In the Holy Spirit, thy Sabbath rest is Thy ark of Thy strength;

For there is rest in the kingdom of God.

Where thy strength of spiritual counsel is, there is reason, wisdom, and

Truth by charity in trust and faith.

In God's power of the Holy Ghost, Thy Kingdom is come.

O, mighty God, our sovereignty.

Thy sovereignty, supremacy and authority are anointed and ordained.

Thy Son, Jesus Christ, is our supremacy.

Thy Holy Ghost is our authority.

Thy will and word are empowered by the Holy Ghost.

Behold thy Sabbath rest is thy salvation and thy strength,

For thy eternal glory is where thy strength remains of the Godhead.

To God be the glory and honor and power where Jesus Christ

Righteousness is thy strength of perfection.

Rejoice, for there is the spirit of sanctity and strength in God's Word,
For thy ways and works are ordained and anointed;
For thy principal power is the unity of the Godhead;
God the Father, God the Son, God the Holy Ghost,
In the beauty of holiness.
All are in one.
God's glory of strength is in thy obedience onto faith,
For the joy of the Lord our God is in faithful sustaining power of Grace and mercy
Where thy saving faith is unto salvation.
In thy virtue, God's promise is faithfully delivered.
In the whole amour of light, thy strength is covered.
In the Spirit, sustainer of healing power is thy strength.
From the softness of grace to the firmness of mercy,
Thy vow of promise is thy word.
God's gift of life is His first strength and first fruit,
For thy life is the gift of strength unto living in God's love for salvation.
Amen.

Jesus Christ is Our Shepherd, Bishop and Savior

Jesus is our Shepherd and Savior of our soul. He is the only Son of God; who faithfully, obediently and perfectly pleased God. His living testaments and scriptural evidences and witnesses are recorded in biblical testimony, words and deeds. Jesus declares unto us simple truths of revelation.

Jesus' revelation gives spiritual significance particularly in the area of spiritual salvation for our soul. For this reason, Jesus says in Psalms 40:7 and Hebrew 10:7, "Then said I, Lo, I come: in the volume of the book *it is* written of me, I delight to do thy will, O my God: yea, thy law is within my Heart". Therefore, our book of the shepherd is the Word of God.

Our Shepherd and Savior of our soul is our gift to eternal salvation. He is the One whom God exalted to His right hand as the "Prince and a Savior, for to give repentance to Israel, and forgiveness of sins" (Acts 5:31 KJV). Jesus is certainly our only divine spiritual gift to eternal life. This gift is certainly in accordance to God's covenant and His provisions which are clearly defined in His office of shepherd-ship. He has divine sovereignty, supremacy, authority and power to enforce, and to direct His creation. We are forever His sheep. God is our Creator who owns His sheep through the redemptive blood of Jesus Christ.

Jesus Christ is our shepherd, who is ordained and appointed to take His part of God's gospel ministry before the beginning of this world from God's Word. Therefore, Jesus springs forth according to God's Word to be approved in one accordance in the unity of God's spirit of life as God's Spirit gives utterance bringing forth His creation to produce His works. Then the shepherd says, "Thou hast made known to me the ways of life; thou shalt make me full of joy with thy countenance" (Acts 2:28 KJV). Immediately, as these things are being done in the spirit of righteousness, the Shepherd exalts our Holy Father who has given Him His circumcision covenants and commandments from the gospel to what is promised through the Holy Spirit in Jesus Christ.

Thus, God's commands are embodied in His spiritual heart and soul produced by His breath He breathes into good works to be done among men with His love as it is in God's kingdom of salvation in heaven. The pastor shepherd always remains accountable and answerable in serving His generations forever. As we are His sheep, our main focus is to continue the good will of God to allow us to faithfully worship Him in spirit and in truth (John 4:24).

The Shepherd comes in order that His flock will be "Praising God, and having favour with all the people. And the Lord added to the church daily such as should be saved" (Acts 2:47 KJV). All these things are done in prayer and supplication with one accord fellowship, but glory, honor and peace is given to every man that faithfully does good works (Rom. 2:10).

Jesus is our Shepherd and Savior of our soul. The king and prophet David truly declares in Psalms 23 this as such:

"The Lord is my Shepherd
I shall not want
He makes me lie down in green pastures;
He leads me beside quiet waters.
He restores my soul;
He guides me in the paths of righteousness
For His name's sake.
Yea though I walk through the
Valley of the Shadow of Death,
I fear no evil, for you are with me;
Your rod and Your staff they comfort me.
You prepare a table before me in
The presence of my enemies;
You have anointed my head with oil;
My cup overflows.
Surely goodness and loving kindness will follow me
All the days of my Life,
And I will dwell in the house of the Lord forever". Amen

Jesus virtually says, "I am the good shepherd. The good shepherd lays down his life for the sheep". (John 10:11) Therefore, Jesus answers all the truths leading to salvation. He answers the question: how to enter the kingdom of salvation saying that you must have belief in the Son who is our Shepherd and Savior of our soul. However, the unbeliever asks, "Who is this Shepherd and who are His sheep?" Therefore, according to this major issue, Jesus confirms again, "I am the good Shepherd, and I know my own and my own know me, even as the Father knows me and I know this Father; and I lay down my life for the sheep" (John 10:14-15 NASB).

Indeed, Jesus' personal statement from the Father declares emphatically and categorically in love identifying who He is. Again, beyond any doubt, Jesus portrays how spiritually significant He is by being the shepherd God sent. Jesus secures the perfect model in how to be the Good Shepherd. He requests His children who are His sheep to become children of God (Rom. 8:16).

In the image of Christ, the children of God become our under shepherds, priests, pastors, ministers, bishops, deacons, teachers, judges or kings by vocation; but God has surely chosen His fold and His course for every shepherd to steward and to shepherd godliness and righteousness in Christ Jesus responsibly. In fact, God declares all who are born of the spirit, are indeed spiritual saints, fathers, mothers of sheep and shepherds in the capacity of disciples trusteeship in being true caregivers and keepers.

In the manner of the true gospel, there are shepherds in the image of Christ today. They come directly from Jesus' authority. Jesus says, "All authority has been given to me in heaven and on earth. Go therefore and make disciples of all the nations, baptizing them in the name of the Father, and the Son and the Holy Spirit, teach them to observe all that I commanded you; and lo, I am with you always even to the end of the age" (Matt. 28:18-20 NASB).

These are God's shepherds from the living rock, our God. They are guardians and keepers of their flocks with all godly regards to protect their flock in all matters. Indeed, every shepherd is his brother's keeper and cultivator of the seed of Christ in every living soul. God's purpose is united in Christ which secures His commands for the salvation of the living souls. These shepherds are loving helpers exercising the will of God (1 Pet. 5:2). For the flocks are "As living stones are being built up as a spiritual house for a holy priesthood to offer up spiritual sacrifice acceptable to God through Christ Jesus" (1 Pet. 2:5 NASB).

What does this mean to be a guardians and keepers of one's flocks doing ministries in all godly regards? Together we are our brother's keeper and guardian in relationship to Christ who is the head of the church. Yes, there are stronger shepherds and there are some weaker shepherds who must stand united against false shepherds. The stronger Christians in their faith must exercise their responsibilities to develop the weaker saints in the faith.

This holds all saints together united in one faith, one love, and in one God. But, in the flesh, Jesus presents His call to the nature of His call of the gospel when He calls unto the Father in His fleshly weakness at Gethsemane. Jesus calls unto the His Father "Abba! Father! All things are possible for you; remove this cup from me; yet not what I will, but what your will" (Mark 14:36 NASB). The love of God's righteous will is for His destination, purpose, and cause that the living church must unite both the weaker saints with the stronger saints all in one spiritual body in Christ. As our Shepherd, Jesus still faithfully demonstrates His weakness in the flesh and His strength in the Spirit only to the point of God's glory when He calls on God and God answers Him in spirit and truth.

Jesus urgently states that it is imperative that believers keep watching and praying that you may not come into temptation. The "Spirit is willing but the flesh is weak" (Mark 14:38 NASB). Salvation is by God's grace effective by Jesus faithfully giving Himself as our sacrifice, in saving faith, and in obedience to the gospel of God's Word (Heb. 9:15).

In the name of Jesus, the church stands upon Jesus Christ's faith our rock, our shepherd and our Savior of our souls by His living Gospel, and He is the author and perfector of faith. Therefore, the spiritual kingdom of God holds our perfect salvation's elect in His perfect sum of members. For this cause, there are many members in the church of God acting on their faith from saints to saints to edify the weaker saints to praise the Lord and to worship God.

The unification of the church is produced there in one body when the shepherds minister to the assemblies as well as the assemblies minister to them according to God's Word. This reciprocal relationship between the shepherds and saints is spiritually significant.

The spirit of the gospel pronounces the church's relationship among all saints in their responsibility unto one another according to whatever the nature, condition and spiritual state in the growth of God. The key principle is Jesus' state of love must be in all the saint's hearts to develop spiritual growth from and between the strongest saints to the weakest saints. This relationship rests upon God's Spirit against the spirit of the flesh. Both the spirit and the flesh emerge where the spirit is the victor and the flesh is in submission. The flesh is in submission, the way Jesus was, calling unto the Father because His Spirit is truly greater in us than the flesh. The spirit is complete in one faith. The spirit both directs and testifies to the flesh in our living soul (2 Cor. 7:1, Gal. 5:17).

The correlation response has spiritual significance showing how the flesh urges its response to the weakness of the soul and how the spirit uplifts the souls. This example illustrates Jesus' walk in the test of temptation. He only relies on the spiritual word of God. Christ demonstrates this example to believers why it is important for believers to care for one another and that they must offer their spiritual love and enrich one another (Matt. 4:4-10, Ps. 35:13).

Jesus' Sacred Body

The anointed living sacrament is Jesus' blood and His bread of life,
For Jesus' sacred body is sanctified and glorified unto God.
As God is glorified through all the kingdoms of God.
In spirit, Jesus' obedience unto God is the virtue of truth,
For Jesus is the light within the light and
He is the light of lights after God's Heart.
The spiritual counsel glories in the true spirit and Word of Life,
For Jesus Christ is ordained by the Holy Ghost in the Holy Spirit.
Full of glory, He is the living image of God and
He testifies truth from the holy crown of glory.
The spirit bears witness to the spirit,
For the spirit speaks truthfully and softly in love.
In one accord, do you hear the spirit speak
Heart to heart from Jesus' sacred body?
There are holy things In Jesus Christ's heavenly body,
For spiritual bodies are sanctified in the body of Jesus Christ.
These bodies shall glorify God in honor and in love.
Living saints of the faith come together united as one in one spirit,
For there is unity in the living Spirit of God.

In the beauty of holiness, God brings all things together.

Jesus Christ's sacred body is the temple of the Holy Spirit.

Who glorifies the ways of God? Where art thou saints?

Are there any witnesses for God today?

Where art thou in worship?

Where is your worthiness in faith?

Whose soul yields unto the light

Let the light of Jesus Christ illuminate thy temple and cleanse thy soul.

Where the Holy Ghost dwells in the consolation of Jesus Christ. Amen.

My Beloved Brethren

Greetings in name of our Holy Father God Jehovah and in the love of God.

God is holy and His love is holy,

For the love of the Holy Ghost is upon you to love God with holy love.

Our soul praises our Holy Father God in worship and prayer.

In the Spirit of God, who art thy brother and thy sister.

To love one another is to have the love of God within you.

Who is your brother's keeper? And is he a lover of God?

In the spirit of love, to know love is to know God and to love God is to love life.

In the kingdom of God, you shall rest in thy holy Sabbath of salvation.

In the law of love, to love God is to love one another.

May God's Holy kiss seal the spirit of virtue on the children of God.

The testimony of faith prays, believes, and heals in love.

Love edifies faith, for there is no need to struggle to be first in the Kingdom of God.

There is the power of faith unto salvation and deliverance.

If you are born of the Spirit of God,

There is no need to be born for adversity and war.

You follow love.

There is no need to be left out when your name is written in the
Book of Life.
There is no need to kill or to murder your brother in the kingdom of God;
For brotherly love puts away the evil discord,
Strife, deceit, hatred, envy and jealousy, betrayal and violence.
There is no objection to God's mercy,
For there is joy in God's mercy and forgiveness.
For my brothers and sisters who do the will of God are
God's beloved chosen.
In one accord, there is honor and love unto our beloved Holy Father, God.
They are my brethren through grace,
For they are heirs to the kingdom of God's salvation.
For they are inspired by God's Spirit of the Holy Ghost.
In the unity of faith, it is good to fellowship and to worship God together,
For we are all brothers and sisters of one people who are of one God.
In brotherly love, there is discipleship, companionship, leadership,
Friendship, fellowship, membership.
And kinship to God for fortification and edification.
There is no hardship in the kingdom of God.
There is unity in the spirit of holiness, loveliness and godliness.
In the spirit of truth, brotherly love bears witness to esteem one another

Greater than oneself.

There is intimacy between God and the saints in the kingdom of God.

Brotherhood has an evangelical spiritual purpose.

There is an invitation to Christ for your enemy and the stranger for the Family of God.

In ministry spirits, brotherly love ministers to your needs.

Brotherly love expresses holy things which are true, pure, and sure.

In the sanctity of truth, God blesses thy brethren to be humbled in Spirit with integrity and charity.

Therefore, love one another as we are to love God and let our hearts be Transformed by the word of

Faith for the manifestation and perfection of sincere love. Amen.

Prayer Dreamer

The prayer dreamer prays in dreams at the altar of grace.
Anointed in God's love, the dreamer beseeches Thee, O Lord.
In the fear of the Lord, the dreamer of prayer prays to honor God's name.
He prays unto God sincerely with spiritual urgency.
In the sanctity of love,
God's name is called to worship Him in the spirit of truth from his heart
Through the ministries of the Holy Ghost,
The prayer dreamer utters the oracles of God through testimonies of faith.
Please God, entreat me to be holy with a right heart and a right spirit.
Grant me Lord to follow you and let your word come into my heart gladly.
Implore me Lord to know your Word and to hear your word effectively.
Let your seed of obedience in faith answers my heart.
May I grow daily in your daily bread through the
Spiritual heart of the seed.
May your trust be pleased of your servant's grace.
May your godliness and loveliness be my comeliness.
I beseech you, Lord, by the meekness of Jesus Christ in the glorious
Gospel;
For my soul inquires of thy Holy Spirit to pray in thy Holy Ghost.
Let the worthiness of my faith be grateful and thankful unto You,
My Lord God.

May the spirit of intercession and forgiveness cover over my oversight.
In the light of Jesus Christ's righteousness, may glory and grace carry me.
In one accord, my soul smiles by thy glory and grace.
The gift of prayer offers a dreamer of prayers with effectual fervent
Prayers of faith to declare the victory of Jesus Christ;
For in my dreams, praying in the Holy Ghost,
I have testified the glory of God in the beauty of holiness.
In the kingdom of God, God's heart is near with holy love.
There in the Spirit of God comes the spirit of prophecy and revelation.
God's glorified virtue reveals the holy light of glory.
The prayer dreamer sees the vision of God's word uncovering the truth of things in the manners of the Spirit of God,
For the Spirit bears witness to the spirit.
Spirit to spirit in truth is by the glory of righteousness through the hope of Jesus Christ.
The joys of spiritual communion with God have sanctified my fasting faith.
I trust you Lord for my sealed prayers which are healed.
The prayer dreamer overflows unto sanctification and glorification.
In the bosom of God, he is lifted up unto the glory of God.
In spirit to spirit, my ears are opened to hear God's words.
Yet, my eyes are closed, but I see the light of glory in God's presence.
I rejoice in our eternal God of pure love and kindness.

In prayer, my ears are closed but I hear resounds of the Spirit speak as Many waters of life.
In prayer, my tongue is sealed, but my mouth speaks reverie of love; Where God places His words in my speech grows from the heart.
In prayer, my touch is healed and revived in the spirit; For the spirit is quickened alive unto a new body of wealth and health.
As a living soul, asleep the wears and care of this world are clothes of the Body who breathe the air of life
But I am clothed in the glory of God, the prayer dreamer. Amen.

Prayer of Deliverance

In the kingdom of God, God hears my prayer of deliverance.
The God of my life who has never forsaken me in my faith.
Sanctify my soul to pray and to praise our Holy Father God.
Hallelujah, praise the name of our Savior, Jesus Christ.
In the Holy Spirit and by the power of the Holy Ghost,
Whose prayer prays for deliverance
In the virtue and grace of Jesus Christ, I ask for this miracle of deliverance.
God glorifies and fortifies this prayer of deliverance.
We are grateful and faithful for your blessings;
For repentance, and deliverance, redemption, reconciliation, and Reformation in the Spirit of God.
In the justification of grace through our Lord and Savior Jesus Christ
Who saves our souls,
My soul prays and praises thy prayer of salvation.
My soul worships and prays in praises unto God our Holy Father
Who is our hope and help.
God is holy and worthy to worship in spirit and truth.
Salvation is thy greatest gift of life in spiritual healings and in praying.
Sanctification with communion in prayer always preaching the Word of God in praise and worship. Faithfully, through the oracles of prayer,

My mouth and heart praise in worship to thy holy

God in His love and faith.

Thank you, heavenly Father God, for Your gift of life.

You are our healer.

For I know the peace of God which is in Jesus' peace.

For You have healed my soul. My soul is healed.

My voice sings joy and praises in the house of God by faith.

Freed from sin and this world of death,

I have victory in the praise of our Lord, Jesus Christ.

My soul is lifted in praise by God's glory and my tears flow with

The glow of glory in joy for you.

Praise the Lord, our God. Holy is thy love for my soul ever thirsts for the

Word of God,

For my beloved God of life, the living God,

Who made me blessed and whole.

My soul is delivered onto God's salvation over the enemy of Satan, sin and

death. Amen.

Salvation

O God, my hope unto eternal life is Thy promise.

God is salvation.

Thou God of my salvation who is my hope unto eternal life.

Deliver me from sin.

You are the power, honor, and glory.

Jesus Christ is my hope and the promised gospel of salvation.

Thy anointed prayers and communion are in faith.

This salvation comes unto you through Christ our Lord and Savior.

Who is thy light and joy?

Salvation is our gift of grace.

Sanctifying the spirit of love by the body of Christ.

In grace and mercy, the Holy Spirit sanctifies thy soul.

To sanctify God's glory is to love God in the communion of the Holy Spirit.

Thy peace is in the unity of truth.

Who is thy author of salvation?

Thou God of my salvation is true. Amen.

The Glory of Holiness

God's holiness sanctifies thy soul unto salvation,

For holiness is the glory of truth through the power of the Holy Ghost.

Holy, holy, holy.

Hosanna, hosanna, hosanna.

Glory hallelujah!

The glory of holiness is the gift of salvation from our Lord, Jesus Christ.

Who is the light of the glory?

Jesus Christ is the glory of holiness in the spirit of godliness,

Loveliness and holiness;

For Jesus Christ is the anointed holy crown and sacred seed of glory.

Who is the God of glory?

Who is the Godhead and the fullness of the glory?

The Alpha and Omega

Emmanuel

The Spirit of God is present,

For there is holiness in the kingdom of God.

God gives us the way of holiness.

We are sanctified in the spirit of holiness.

Through holiness, we praise and honor God in prayer and worship,

For all things of holiness are joined and

Sealed together with integrity of faith.

We are saints of sanctification and glorification in Jesus Christ's
Compassion and love,
For holiness is the living light of God filled in the Holy Ghost through our
Lord, Jesus Christ.
For the glory of holiness is the testimony of Jesus Christ from
His spiritual sacrifices.
Jesus Christ is the light who removes the shadow of death.
Therefore, we are holy in our Lord and Savior Jesus Christ.
You are holy saints in the fear of the Lord.
Holiness, godliness, and loveliness are purified and
Glorified in our present beings of glory,
For the Word of God is the Holy Spirit.
And the spirit is the heart of the seed.
There the spirit and the Word come into the glory of holiness.
God gives us all the spiritual keys of the holy knowledge of holiness
And godliness,
For God is holy.
We are heirs of salvation in the kingdom of God.
There is wealth in the spirit and the riches of glory.
Giving God the glory, there is health for your mind in the Spirit of God.
We are forgiven of all our sins and given the gift of the Holy Spirit;
Living saved, sanctified, and glorified.
Sow in the spirit and reap in the fruit of the Word by praying,

Praising and worshiping God.

In the beauty of holiness, Jesus Christ is the light of glory and
He is the spirit of loveliness.

There is unity in the spirit of holiness and truth.

We are saved through Jesus Christ's righteousness unto the gift of
Salvation.

Our spirit and soul are summoned in the manner of holiness.

Thy holiness glows in all holy things which are true, pure, and sure.

In God's love from sanctification unto glorification, we have salvation.

Sow the word and reap loveliness. Sow obedience and reap faith.

Sow compassion and reap lowliness. Sow belief and reap salvation.

Sow grace and reap mercy. Sow faith and reap courage in the will of God.

Sow love and reap the love of God.

Sow holiness and reap a holy life.

Sow loveliness and reap godliness.

Sow kindness and gentleness and reap loyalty and reliability.

Sow temperance and reap a calm spirit.

Let our heart and tongue be from the Lord, our God.

Sow God's law and reap the letter. Sow justice and reap mercy.

Sow healing and reap wholeness. Sow integrity and reap character.

Sow tenacity and reap destiny. Sow identity and reap personality.

Sow honesty and reap a humbled spirit. Sow liberty and reap creativity.

Sow fidelity and reap charity. Sow sincerity and reap responsibility.

Sow accountability and reap authority in the name of Jesus Christ.
Sow ingenuity and reap dignity. Sow humility and reap stability.
Sow maturity and reap fertility. But sow enmity and reap vanity.
Sow iniquity and reap insincerity. Sow depravity and reap guilty thinking.
But, sowing the sanctity of God is the credibility of true love
In the glory of holiness,
For God's Spirit of inspirational truth rises from
His glory of godliness and holiness.
Through the ministry of holiness,
God's Word of Truth is sanctified in our hearts,
For thy edification and comfort in God is to obey in faith.
The circumcised heart is a heart of transformation by the word of faith.
Obedience in faith is the ministry of holiness,
For the glory of holiness reaches and teaches in the spirit of truth.
Let us rejoice in the spirit of truth and the
Spirit of righteousness of Jesus Christ,
For God's holy presence is near.
For God is with us in the body of Jesus Christ.
Emmanuel.
The Holy Spirit quickens and overflows in God's glory of holiness.
There is reverence in our adoration of grace.
We have repentance unto forgiveness in the gratitude of grace.
In the promise of salvation,

We are saved to worship God in spirit and truth,

For there is honor for the God of glory.

We shall bless God's holy name with our soul and spirit,

For we know God's anointing is ordained by God's love and His glory.

Surely, we believe in our Lord Savior Jesus Christ.

Truly, we know God is our joy and hope.

We are restored and we are made whole.

Purely, we are blessed to have God's peace and comfort,

For all these things are covered by God's glory unto salvation.

This is the law of truth and grace to magnify God's name and to sanctify

His love in our hearts by God's glory of holiness. Amen.

The Joy of God's Glory

The joy of God's glory rests in His love for you and me
Because He is love.
For the kingdom of God is the gift to life.
Holy, holy, holy is our God of life.
For the joy of the Lord, our God, are His heirs to the kingdom of salvation.
We bless His holy name in the prayers of honor, mercy, and grace;
For the joy of God's glory inspires your living and breathing soul.
And His joy of hope magnifies and anoints
My spirit through the Holy Spirit.
Hallelujah.
This incredible and irresistible grace moves my spirit.
My spiritual faith increases by the testimonies of God's word.
His word of glory lives in my heart by His faith of righteousness.
Ever increasing faith living by every word of God bears good fruit.
Hallelujah.
Glory to glory
And spirit to spirit in truth.
The kingdom of God is near,
For there is a place for you and me in the kingdom of God
In the spirit of liberty, my soul is called and my spirit is summoned in faith.
My soul offers prayers, praises and worship holding on to the Word of Life.

In the spirit of truth, we freely worship God by the gift of life;
For God is the glory and the honor and the power.
He is the light of glory.
And the beauty of holiness and the spirit of loveliness.
His eternal glory is justified by faith.
To know we are His heirs of salvation unto eternal glory is to know our
Savior, Jesus Christ;
For He is our Bishop and Savior of our soul in the spirit of grace.
Through the spirit of love and grace, we are redeemed and
Forgiven from our great sins of death and disobedience.
In the glory of God,
We are lifted up in His bosom and carried beyond the heavens.
We are thankful and gratified and sanctified and
Purified and edified and fortified
From the gift of God's glory to fortification, to gratification,
Sanctification and edification, justification and glorification.
Where we are in the body of Christ, there we are saved,
Sanctified and glorified.
Holy, holy, holy;
For God is our salvation and our glory.
No longer will we see in closed fleshly eyes but now
Through our faith in eternal glory and spiritual salvation.
Thank you Jesus Christ our Lord and Savior. Amen.

The Preached Word

The preached word must not be breached,
For the blessed word is delivered by the Holy Ghost in the Spirit of God.
The sheep are awakened from their sleep in a day to pray.
They are very meek to know how to seek
God first in faith in the kingdom of God.
Faithful sheep jump and leap in faith with the hope of
Jesus Christ's righteousness.
They pay heed to know their need and they know who keeps their
Salvation.
Not to bleed their deed or bleed the feed.
All of God's sheep know they are heirs of salvation who
Hold on deep to every word of God.
They hear and obey with all diligence, who listen and follow with
Obedience and faith.
Their defense is God's spiritual word in full feed from the seed of life,
For God is their sustainer;
Who sows and reaps in the joy of holiness and loveliness.
The kingdom of God is near and there is never a time to weep,
For God is near. Amen.

The Sacred Elect Elders

Behold, the Sabbath day of the Lord, our God, is glorified in charity.
Charity is the commandment of love and it is sanctified by the Holy Ghost,
For God is Love.
Through the gift of love, mercy and grace,
God represents charity in godliness.
There is charity in the gift of the sacred elect elders.
They are our godly men known in our fathers, sons,
Uncles, brothers and nephews.
In holiness, the sacred elect elders are ordained and anointed as godly
Men after God's own heart.
These men are God's selected chosen who study and watch
God's word diligently.
As God's word nurtures and builds lives for the kingdom of God,
His heavenly eye remains on them.
The sacred elect elders are called to minister to God and
To the people of grace.
Eminent in the power of the Holy Ghost and the power of God,
These men and women of God are united as one to esteem
One another in love.
They stand out as God's elect elders to fulfill generation to generation
From edification to sanctification.

In the spirit of love, their ministries of charity build and edify the body of
Jesus Christ after God's own heart,
For charity is in the heart of love;
Where the Holy Ghost dwells in thy holy temple of grace and mercy.
Behold, salvation is revealed by truth in the beauty of holiness.
This is our gift of hope through our Lord Jesus Christ, for God is love.
The Holy Ghost anoints godly men in God's name to obey,
To serve, to watch and to honor God in love with honest hearts;
For charity serves love in kindness and in adorations and affection
For the good will of God.
In every hour, watch, they have the spirit of thanksgivings and
Praises to offer God as they worship God in the spirit of liberty.
Prayer never ceased for the godly men as they minister to
God and to the people.
They prayed in God's presence.
It is easy to see the things of God when you stand near thy holiness.
God is love and His witness and testimony are true,
For these godly men refresh their spirit in the covenant of love.
They are bound to God to represent pure love and holiness for they are
Holy men of God.
They know the virtue of God's strength is godly love.
They know loving one another brings glory to God.
They know holiness and charity are pure gifts of love

In the kingdom of God where hearts are opened and
Secrets of the hearts are manifested in thy worthiness of faith.
Do you have need to be healed?
Do you have need to be relieved?
Do you have need to be believed?
For God's truths are revealed through the spirit of revelation.
Godly men clearly worship God making intercession for all godly things.
Blessed be your soul and spirit which are considered with godly valor and
Virtue for God.
Godly men believe in God to offer prayers of consolation for
Restoration and reconciliation.
In the glory of God, charity speaks through the gift of the
Spirit to edify and to exhort: preaching, reaching and teaching in the spirit.
The sacred elect elders offer their obedience to acknowledge
God's power in His word and His deeds. God holds peace in godly order.
God knows godly men are on one accord as heaven echoes and the earth
Resounds.
Their hearts are to heart in the knowledge of the hearts to witness the
Beauty of holiness,
For the strength of a man is God's Spirit and God's Word.
For the Holy Ghost teaches men in spiritual things.
These men spiritually discern the Spirit of God to intercede for
Others in behalf of their soul that God meet their needs.

In prayer, they bring all things together for the will of God.
They are praying for healing in reconciling. They are hearing and obeying
God's word.
They are sharing and caring with heart's compassion,
For their faith is our example of Christ in words and deeds.
In the sanctity of life, Jesus Christ is our hope and redemption.
For godly men are giving and forgiving.
They are hoping and trusting God for liberty and deliverance.
They are loving and being loved by God.
They are walking and talking by faith.
They are seeing and touching love by faith.
Surely, they are believing and trusting in God.
God's love is calling your name.
Your heart's ears hear this call to obey His soft spoken
Words of deliverance.
From heart to heart and face to face, we live by grace and faith;
For the joy of the lord is our strength.
The elder's prayers have been heard by God to cure our wounds of hurt.
God forgives our sin transgression through prayer.
Thanks be to God for the communion of prayer to hear our call.
When we are cleansed, we bear the image of God with the
Right spirit of grace for His godliness.
The light of God shines through godly men, for they are children of God;

For godly men worship and praise God with sacred hearts.
Godly men honor and obey God both in body and in spirit.
Inspired godly men have personal relationship with
God in spiritual intimacy.
There is spiritual identity in prayer through our lord Jesus Christ
With spiritual significance.
In the glory of God, godly men manifest manifold wisdom of God through
The touch of grace in valor and virtue.
To worship God holy in spirit and truth is to love God true and pure.
Godly men acknowledge God's sovereignty: God the Father,
And the Holy Ghost's authority and Jesus Christ the supremacy.
Therefore, God's glorified virtue is magnified and fortified in the mighty
Strength of the Holy Spirit.
Through God's glorified virtue, God is love.
We watch and pray knowing salvation is removed from
Impurity and impiety, insolence and insurrection of disobedience.
Shielded by God's grace, godly men are safe and sound,
Stable and secure in heart.
There is fellowship intimacy in God through our Lord Jesus Christ,
For godly men come between God's righteousness and His mighty wrath
By prayer.
Who praise God for being God and walk as men of God
Free of envy and strike and division.

To serve God is to believe in Him and to know Him by your faith.

Do you know God today, here and now?

To know God is to love God. Amen.

We honestly serve God by our believing faith and our honoring Him.

We watch against the evil one knowing Christ has the victory already.

We are trusting God will guide us with His eye.

God will watch us between Him and us.

As godly men consider their ways to follow after the righteousness of Jesus Christ, so do we; for they have been our great examples.

We trust God whole heartedly in the faith.

We are empowered by God's will with all our needs met.

God's valor and virtue shower us in daily blessings of grace according to His heart, for godly men are God's jewel and crown of His glory in the Spirit of God.

Behold, charity reveals honor and peace through the light of glory.

Charity relieves and receives and gives the required need.

Who perceive their needs today and have ears to hear and eyes to see

Knowing God is in the spirit of truth,

For the light of their eyes shine with enthusiasm for the unity of the faith

By the Spirit of God.

The sacred elect elders retain honor and integrity through Jesus Christ as
They give God love and charity,
For the Holy Ghost ministers through godly men of charity who are holy
And godly in the image of God.
Godly men are humble souls of grace who please God.
They are God's beloved elect,
Who are ever obeying and believing in the holy things of
God having fasting faith in abstaining from all sin and
All evil through Jesus Christ.
We thank God for our sacred elect elders being godly men of valor and
Virtue unto the gift of God. Amen.

The Soul Keeper

Jesus Christ is our Bishop and Savior of our soul.

I am the Messiah; thy soul keeper.

I am the Son of God from above,

For the Holy Ghost is the sanctifier of thy soul.

Blessed is He who is thy soul keeper.

God's gift to us is our soul.

In the kingdom of God, God is the keeper of our souls.

I am the Bread of Life.

In the kingdom of God, there are sanctified and glorified souls;

For the Lord is thy keeper of your souls.

In the will of God, the soul is given to worship God and salvation is God's Eternal gift.

Whose souls are anointed and freed in the spirit of liberty,

For thy soul prays spiritual prayers in fasting grace.

For thy soul loves the Lord, our God in holiness, loveliness, and godliness.

We shall bless the Lord, our God deeply from our soul.

Humble souls are redeemed, restored and reconciled.

To know God is to love God.

But the sin of disobedience is the curse of death and there is a place for Souls who follow Satan.

Souls in judgment and hell which are Satan's.

The fellowship of God is for righteousness and obedience unto thy faith.

The heart of the soul is the spirit;

Souls unto the Word of God, are the gift of salvation.

I am the way, the truth and the life.

Soul salvation is the glory of the Lord.

Saints of glory,

I am the Alpha and Omega who is thy soul keeper

Giving Your All to Christ

When you give your all
And you have given up to impatience
And lose faith against truth
And gave way to the winds
And to the waves of sin,
God calls repentance for your soul and
Deliverance comes.
Now, God calls you out of your cave;
The death tomb.
As a slave to sin,
You died
But quickened in spirit.
You live in bravery
And boldness in the Word.
A victor in Jesus' grace
Where all your needs are met.
To whom much is given,
Much is required.
There is holiness in bravery
Over sin in slavery. Amen.

Inheritance

God's inheritance for His heirs are living blessings.

In the kingdom of God, kingdom heirs hold on to the integrity of faith.

We are saints.

We are holding on to Jesus' garment.

Tenacity holds on.

We are children of God who are whole, complete and perfect by Jesus' blood.

We, now, are heirs of salvation.

In the glory of holiness, where the beauty of holiness remains in Jesus Christ.

Sustaining love in the Spirit of the living God, our Lord and Savior, Jesus Christ is life.

Hallelujah.

The kingdom of God is near.

Hold on to the hem of Jesus' garment.

Do I lift up thy prayers unto He who draws us near?

The kingdom of glory,

For the glory of God is revealed in the beauty of holiness.

The seed of the word remains.

Pour into my soul, Lord, Your sweet anointing substances;

For the joy of God's strength is His salvation.

Fill me with the Holy Ghost.

Grant my soul to rejoice in thy gift of salvation.

If by Your will, Your ways, Your words and works testify the truth.

Please bear witness in my life to trust in You and believe in Your truth by Your Spirit.

Then I shall rest in Thy calmness and ease.

Prepare my heart and I will hear thy voice, O God, within my heart.

My faith, trust and obedience are unto You; my joy, my God.

Where I give God fruit unto Thy Word I am blessed.

The holy God gives salvation freely.

We shall rest in reliance and assurance of faith.

To please Thee, O God, is to have faith and obedience.

In spirit and truth, we worship You

For you sow the seed of the Word in spirit.

Lead me, Lord. Repent thy soul.

Wash me and cleanse my mind and soul by Your glory,

For my soul desires to praise my God.

My spirit seeks Thee first.

Morning grace, spring me up in Thy living water.

The fire of the Holy Ghost guides me in Thy path.

These majestic blessings anoint my soul.

Ordain my mouth in Thy truth as You call me unto deliverance.

Thank you, heavenly Father, God.

Here I am. Know my heart to serve and to worship You in godliness and Holiness.

Amen.

God's Holy Glory

Holy is the glory of God.

Holy, holy, holy is God's glory.

Through our Lord and Savior Jesus Christ.

Glory is thy virtue from the Holy Ghost.

In the glory of God, holy is Thy name.

Which is full of Thy glory.

Faithful is the eternal love of God.

Thy love nourishes and glories through Thy shield of grace,

For the light of God's glory shines from glory to glory.

Who glows in the spirit of truth and in the Spirit of the Holy Ghost.

Truth to truth flows from love to love.

God is love.

God's love is in the kingdom of God

For God is the glory.

God's glory is the beauty of holiness.

The kingdom of glory is God's grace and mercy.

That His glory passes over me and fills me unto His vessel of honor

By the faithful word of Jesus Christ's gospel of grace.

Repent and come near unto God and His glory shall appear.

To live in God's glorification and fortification is to live in God's glory.

To know God's glory is to know His sovereignty, supremacy and authority;
For God's knowledge of His sovereignty is His glory.
For God's glory is thy Word and will.
Thy eternal glory remains in thy Godhead. To God be the glory.
The spirit of sanctity is full of God's glory in the righteousness and Holiness of Jesus Christ,
That our true obedience and faith is God's glory,
That God's love is the joy of His glory.
Therefore, let the joy of God's glory inspire thy spirit. Amen.

Blessed Healing Grace

Blessed is thy soul who is healed.

Healing grace is blessed in the spirit of liberty.

The Word of God lives through thy precepts and thy doctrine of love.

In the kingdom of God, blessed healing grace covers thy soul.

In healing faith, God's law of love is perpetual healings, kindness and Charity.

In healing faith, there are love bonds in communion to God to know our Obligation unto His will by divine grace for the sanctity of love.

The sanctity of love answers thy faith in the fear of the Lord, my God.

Who in the fear of the Lord, my God.

Who freely yields obedience in the bonds of faith.

Jesus touches my soul with sacred healings.

My soul is delivered by faith in Jesus.

For we know that these sacred healings are by faith in the Lord, our God;

Who is through the gift of the Holy Spirit the power of glory;

For my soul loves my God, our Holy Father of heaven and earth and Heavenly places in Jesus Christ.

This is with all my heart and being in spirit and breath and soul's Substance,

The anointing of Jesus' Holy Spirit who touches me.

He touches from God's holy throne in the power of healing grace,
For the love of God has the authority and power to heal
For God's gift to heal is sanctified.
The gift of God is to cleanse from sin, to mend and to forgive,
To reconcile and to restore
Fellowship for my eternal soul and spirit.
This is amazing grace to praise God for His holy name,
For His holy name yields the fruits of praise on our lips in prayers of Thankfulness.
Let my soul be His vessel of praise to honor and draw me nearer unto You, Lord that my soul may be united in Thee.
For we know Jesus' faith is our salvation for your soul.
He is our Savior and Bishop of our soul.
Delightfully, humble my soul, my God, in the beauty of holiness.
Let this soul be humbled and faithfully delivered by Your will.
Repent and cleanse my heart and prepare my heart to love You in my spirit.
May You grant this prayer of healing grace and mercy in the Holy Spirit of Jesus Christ For His blessed healings that heal thy soul.
My joy is whole.
I worship You truthfully and freely in Your love forever our beloved Savior. Amen.

Heirs of Salvation

Praise God my soul is saved.

I am preserved and made whole.

Freely, God is my salvation. I am delivered.

Blessed is eternal salvation in God,

For salvation comes unto you

In God's eternal glory and honor,

By His faithful words of grace

For your faithfulness is Jesus Christ

Our Lord and Savior of our souls.

Our soul of salvation is freed in Christ.

I am freed and delivered.

Repentance to salvation for deliverance

From sin and death.

Jesus is the way, the truth, the light and the life

To the light and hope of salvation;

For faith in salvation is faith in Jesus' righteousness.

The way of salvation is the gift of life in the Word of God.

Thy faith believes in the power of God.

The Gospel of Jesus Christ is the power unto salvation by God, our Father.

I will rejoice in Jesus' salvation.

God's spirit of love and joy, peace, goodness, meekness.

Who is my help?

The word of salvation draws from the wells of salvation.

In the fear of the Lord, who is the strength of my salvation.

We worship in the spirit and truth

In thy salvation with holiness.

Salvation is through Jesus Christ;

Our salvation covenant

For we are heirs of salvation.

Amen.

Holy Love

Behold, my beloved

God's love is revealed.

God is love.

His reverence fills our souls.

Holy love is given unto us.

And His gift gives reverence to worship God, our Holy Father.

He who loves my soul is He who knows my soul.

My soul loves our Holy Father.

I am so pleased to witness and to worship truly and freely.

The children of God give greatly in praises and thanksgivings for

His holy love.

His holy love is given unto me for my salvation.

His holy love is my forgiveness over sin to cleanse my soul from evil.

We are freed and cleansed.

In the sanctity of holy love, I am redeemed and restored.

I belong to Christ who anoints holy love by the Holy Spirit

In the grace of God,

For God's holy love.

Amen.

Logos

The Word of the Lord speaks

Thy safeguards as a mighty sword,

For the fear of the Lord is the beginning of knowledge.

The Words of the Lord

Are pure words as silver;

Tried in a furnace of earth.

In prayer, the Word shields and nourishes thy soul.

The Word answers above the nights and days.

His Word enlightens and defends.

His Sprit, is from above, is life's preserver cord

For all thy substance.

Thy Word calls,

"Abide thou with me,

Fear not: for he that seeketh my life

Seeketh thy life: but with me

Thou shalt be in safeguard" (2 Sam 22:23 KJV).

I love thee

Your Safeguard from fear

I am your sanctuary

"...For there is peace to thee, and no hurt;

As the Lord liveth" (1 Sam. 20:21 KJV).

Thy Word is God.

From the Word of Truth and spirit in Jesus Christ. Amen.

God is Love

A

Love prayer

To whom God

Has blessed you with many gifts and life.

This

Is love

And love shall be

By showing and praying to God for guidance, forgiveness

And being blessed to do

God's will.

For

God will

Protect, bless and guide

You forever and ever

With love

Forever

For

God is love

And shall be forever

And may you remember to

Love and pray

God

Is with you

And your family

To fight your battles

Forever

Always

May

God give many blessings

To you and I and your

Family and everyone

With love

In

God is love,

And we love,

And He shall bring forth

Many blessed days ahead

We

Thank God for everything

And blessed to be serving Him forever,

And ever

Amen

Alphabetical Poem Listing

A Faithful Hearer of God's Word Listens Obediently, 157

A Kiss in the Rain, 142

A Mother's Prayer on Mother's Day, 167

A Testimony in Crisis and Calling for God's Deliverance, 22

Blessed Healing Grace, 232

Christian Suffrage in Spiritual Significance, 87

Christmas Prayer, 162

Elect Lady, 33

Fasting Faith, 165

Gifted Children, 56

Giving Your All to Christ, 226

God is Love, 239

God is Our Lord, 58

God is the Glory, 129

God Our Holy Father, 106

God the Holy Ghost is our Authority of Justice, 67

God's Gift of Holy Faith, 41

God's Gift of Praise, 120

God's Gift of the Church, 25

God's Glory of Restoration, 185

God's Glory of Strength, 188

God's Heart is Near, 57

God's Holy Gift, 147

God's Holy Glory, 230

God's Holy Love, 70

God's Holy Passover Prayer, 126

God's Holy Spirit of Ministries Worship, 65

God's Temple Endures Satan's Temptation, 140

God's Gift of Hope, 159

God's Glorified Virtue, 103

God's Holy Light of Glory, 152

God's Wisdom Speaks, 115

Grace's Covenant, 56

Hallelujah, 43

Heirs of Salvation, 234

Holy, 61

Holy Anointed Oil, 45

Holy Fire of the Holy Ghost, 113

Holy Love, 236

I Know Secrets, 144

I, Too, Feel the Colours of the Wind, 72

In The Image of God, 29

Inheritance, 227

Jesus Breathes, 27

Jesus Christ is Our Shepherd, Bishop and Savior, 190

Jesus is the Way of the Spirit, 155

Jesus' Sacred Body, 198

Justice, 63

Life's Interlude, 128

Logos, 237

My Beloved Brethren, 200

My Holy Father, My God, 47

My Soul Praises, 98

Prayer, 154

Prayer Dreamer, 203

Prayer of Deliverance, 206

Rainbows of Fruit, 181

Salvation, 208

Salvation is God's Gift to the Church, 80

Sin's Season, 83

Spirit of Intercession, 74

Spirit of Liberty, 117

Spirit of the Word, 89

Tears of My Overflow, 77

The Anointed of the Holy Spirit, 137

The Anointed Touch, 81

The Beauty of Holiness, 31

The Blessings of Our Heavenly Father, 35

The Circumcised Heart, 180

The Eye of Pride, 85

The Father I Pray To Be, 135

The Father's Prayer, 108

The Gift of Living Waters, 48

The Gift of the Church, 39

The Glory of Holiness, 209

The Glory of the Gospel, 20

The Good Fight of Faith, 150

The Heart of Circumcision, 179

The Holy Kiss of the Holy Ghost, 52

The Holy Resurrection of Glory, 54

The Holy Seed of the Holy Ghost, 122

The Joy of God's Glory, 214

The Lamb of God, 37

The Ministry of Miracles, 100

The Ministry of the Holy Ghost, 50

The Mother of Life, 92

The Pastor's Wife, 145

The Prayer of Faith, 111

The Preached Word, 216

The Sacred Elect Elders, 217

The Seasons of Love, 79

The Soul Keeper, 224

The Spirit of Father's Day, 133

The Spirit of Hospitality, 95

The Virtuous Woman, 173

Time, 176

Who is the Shepherd and Savior of our Soul?, 182

Biography

Minister Joseph Phillips Jr., M. Th. was born in Detroit, Michigan to Doris Mary Brantley and Joseph Phillips, Sr. in 1956.

Previously, Joseph studied under Bishop Alexander Jones of Jones Temple Church of God in Christ in Hamtramck, Michigan. Currently, Minister Philips is a member of Evangel Church of God in Christ under the leadership of Pastor Superintendent James Smith Jr. where Joseph faithfully assists in the preparation and direction of the religious worship services both in the Word and music ministries. Ordained by God, Joseph is equipped and established in the Word of God.

Joseph and his beloved godly wife, Victoria Ann Smith Phillips, are blessed with eight children combined.

Joseph holds an Associate of Religious Education Degree from the Family Radio School of the Bible of Oakland, California. Additionally, he holds a Bachelor of Political Science from Wayne State University, Detroit, Michigan and a Master of Theology degree from the Christian Bible College of Rocky Mount, North Carolina.

Joseph's desire is to esteem others in God's love and His word for the spiritual guidance concerning one's promise in faith.

www.ingramcontent.com/pod-product-compliance
Lightning Source LLC
Chambersburg PA
CBHW020646300426
44112CB00007B/265